P9-DTR-477

The Passion of Jesus
in the
Gospel of Luke

· exlibris ·

Mark
McVann, FSC

The Passion Series

Volume 3

The Passion of Jesus in the Gospel of Luke

by

Donald Senior, C.P.

Michael Glazier
Wilmington, Delaware

About the Author

Donald Senior, C.P., is Professor of New Testament at Catholic Theological Union in Chicago. He has written well and extensively on biblical subjects. Among his publications are *The Passion of Jesus in the Gospel of Mark; The Passion of Jesus in the Gospel of Matthew* and *1 & 2 Peter*, volume 20 of the New Testament Messsage series, of which he is co-editor. He is also a book review editor for *The Catholic Biblical Quarterly*.

First published in 1989 by Michael Glazier, Inc., 1935 West Fourth Street, Wilmington, Delaware 19805.

Copyright ©1989 by Michael Glazier, Inc. All rights reserved.

No part of this publication may be reproduced or transmitted in any form or by any means, electronic or mechanical, including photocopy, recording, or any information storage and retrieval system, without permission in writing from the publisher: Michael Glazier, 1935 West Fourth Street, Wilmington, Delaware, 19805.

Library of Congress Cataloging in Publication Data
Senior, Donald.
    The passion of Jesus in the Gospel of Luke.

    (Passion series; 3)
    Bibliography: p.
    Includes index.
    1. Jesus Christ—Passion—Biblical teaching.
2. Jesus Christ—Resurrection—Biblical teaching.
3. Bible. N.T. Luke—Criticism, interpretation, etc.
I. Title. II. Series: Senior, Donald. Passion series; 3.
BT431.S45 1988   226'.406   88-82470
ISBN 0-89453-461-0

Typography by Angela Meades.
Printed in the United States of America.

Contents

PREFACE

With this volume on Luke, the Passion Series approaches a Gospel that has special appeal in the suffering churches of the world. Luke presents a Jesus who is attuned to the voice of the poor and marginalized, a Jesus whose message of justice is proclaimed with a sharp prophetic edge. It is also a Gospel where the experiences of rejection and brutal death loom large. Whether one belongs to a martyr church or not, the message of this Gospel needs to be heard today with unflinching attention. A close reading of the Passion of Jesus according to Luke draws one into the heart of his challenging theology.

As in the first two volumes of this series, the intent is to bring the insights of biblical scholarship to a wider audience, hopefully without sacrificing either subtlety or clarity.[1] In the case of Luke's Passion narrative, scholarship has been particularly active in recent years. In the United States, a number of books devoted exclusively to Luke's Passion have appeared, and European scholarship has also been active on this subject.[2] While I will draw on all of these contributions,

---

[1]See D. Senior, C.P., *The Passion of Jesus in the Gospel of Mark* (Wilmington: Michael Glazier, 1984); *The Passion of Jesus in the Gospel of Matthew* (Wilmington: Michael Glazier, 1985). The volume on John is forthcoming.

[2]Among American scholars see, for example, R. Karris, *Luke: Artist and Theologian* (New York: Paulist, 1985); J. Neyrey, *The Passion According to Luke: A Redaction Study of Luke's Soteriology* (New York: Paulist, 1985); J.B. Tyson, *The Death of Jesus in Luke-Acts* (Columbia: University of South Carolina, 1986); M. Soards, *The Passion According to Luke: The Special Material of Luke 23* (Sheffield: JSOT Press, 1987). The works of F. Matera, *Passion Narratives and Gospel Theo-*

I hope my own work will not be redundant. Few of these recent efforts attempt the approach of this series—namely, to comment on the full span of Luke's Passion story in the light of his entire Gospel (and in Luke's case, the Acts of the Apostles).[3]

Part of the reason for all this attention is this Gospel's special appeal for an age in which questions of economic justice, peace, and the prophetic role of the churches—questions all important in Luke—are so urgent. But scholars have also been drawn to a study of Luke because of other questions intrinsic to this Gospel. First of all, Luke is the only evangelist to couple a story of the church directly to his narrative about Jesus. In the cases of Mark, Matthew, and John, one can only make educated guesses about their vision of the church, but through the Acts of the Apostles Luke has elaborated his vision for all to see. Modern biblical scholarship has been increasingly absorbed by the essential relationship between Luke's two volumes, and no study of the Gospel (including this one) can afford to ignore how Luke carries through the colors and tones of his portrayal of Jesus into his presentation of the early church.[4]

The special interest of recent biblical scholarship in the literary qualities of the Gospels also leads it to focus on Luke. Using the tools of literary criticism, biblical scholars have appreciated, as perhaps never before, the power of

logies (New York: Paulist, 1986) and J. Massyngbaerde Ford, *My Enemy is My Guest* (Maryknoll: Orbis, 1984) also give substantial attention to Luke's Passion narrative. In Europe the important works of A. Büchele, *Der Tod Jesu im Lukasevangelium* (Frankfurt: Knecht, 1978) and F. Untergassmair, *Kreuzweg und Kreuzingung Jesu* (Paderborn: Schöningh, 1980) should be mentioned. To individual monographs have been added a host of other studies and commentaries; particularly important in the latter category are the works of J. Fitzmyer, *The Gospel According to Luke X-XXIV* (Anchor Bible 28A; New York: Doubleday, 1985) and I. Howard Marshall, *Commentary on Luke* (New International Greek Testament Commentary; Grand Rapids: Eerdmans, 1978).

[3]Most of these authors focus on major scenes (e.g., Neyrey, Ford, Tyson) or portions of Luke's narrative (e.g., Karris and Büchele focus on chapter 23, Soards on chapter 22).

[4]This is a particular emphasis of J. Neyrey in his work on Luke's soteriology. See also J. Tyson, *The Death of Jesus*, and R. Tannehill, *The Narrative Unity of Luke-Acts* (Philadelphia: Fortress, 1986).

narrative and have studied the intricate and subtle dynamics in play between a literary text and its reader. Of all the evangelists Luke may have the greatest skills as a narrator. His two volume work brims with artful stories, parables, and epic scenes, some of which draw upon motifs and rhetorical devices of the first century Mediterranean world. The Passion story is no exception to this and several recent studies have focused upon the literary qualities of Luke's Passion.[5] In our analysis of Luke, attention to the literary qualities of the Passion story will be one of several focal points.

Another source of Luke's magnetism for recent scholarship is the challenge his Passion story raises for discovering the sources of his Gospel. When it comes to narrating the Passion of Jesus, Matthew and Mark are identical with each other in the sequence of events. And even though each evangelist puts his own characteristic stamp on his narrative, it is clear that one is dependent on the other. In my study of Matthew, I argued that Matthew was dependent on Mark and needed no other significant source in shaping his own Passion story. Those passages that are unique to Matthew (such as the death of Judas, Mt 27:2-10) or Pilate's washing of his hands (Mt 27:24-25) were elaborated by the evangelist from leads in Mark's account and from the inspiration of his own theology and community traditions.[6]

But in the case of Luke, changes of order in the sequence of events and more notable deviations from the story line established by Mark (and followed by Matthew) have led some scholars to suggest that Luke had access to another major source for his Passion story other than that of the Gospel of Mark.[7] For example, in Luke the anointing story

[5]See, for example, R. Karris, *Luke: Artist and Theologian*, who traces Luke's literary artistry in selected themes of the Gospel, finding their resolution in chapter 23, and R. Tannehill, *The Narrative Unity of Luke-Acts*.

[6]D. Senior, *The Passion of Jesus in the Gospel of Matthew*; also, "Matthew's Special Material in the Passion Story: Implications for the Evangelist's Redactional Technique and Theological Perspective," in *Ephemerides Theologicae Lovanienses*— 63 (1987) 272-94.

[7]See especially. V. Taylor, *The Passion Narrative of St Luke: A Critical and Historical Investigation* (ed. O. Evans; Cambridge: University Press, 1972). In his

takes place not in the context of the Passion but earlier in the midst of Jesus' public ministry (see 7:36-50); the supper scene includes a farewell discourse of Jesus to his apostles (22:14-38); the mockery of Jesus precedes rather than follows his interrogation by the Sanhedrin (22:63-65), while the mockery by the Roman soldiers at the trial is dropped altogether. And Luke's account is enriched with scenes not found in Mark or Matthew, such as the appearance before Herod (23:6-16), Jesus' address to the women of Jerusalem (23:27-31) and the repentance of the Good Criminal (23:39-43).

While the suggestion that Luke had a special source for his Passion story is a seductive one, my own opinion is that the special character of Luke's Passion narrative is due to his creative reinterpretation of Mark's account.[8] In fact, this is true throughout the Gospel of Luke. Using the materials provided by Mark and a collection of Jesus' sayings (called the "Q source") that Luke shares in common with Matthew, the evangelist created his own distinctive portrayal of Jesus and his message. Certainly inspiration for Luke's distinctive view came from currents within his community: ways of understanding Jesus and his mission, ways of celebrating and understanding the Eucharist, stories that developed around the memory of Jesus, and so on. But such resources were not in the form of a cohesive Passion story different from that of Mark's Gospel. While Luke may have been bolder than Matthew in his distinctive rendering of the Passion, his major literary sources are, therefore, no different. What does differ is that Luke writes from and for a Christian community whose experiences are necessarily distinct from those of the communities of Mark and Matthew. And so his

view Luke's Passion narrative was preceded by a "proto-Luke," that is, a version of the Passion story independent of that of Mark. The evangelist Luke would have created the version in his Gospel by blending proto-Luke and the Markan Passion story.

[8]Therefore analogous to what Matthew does in composing his Passion narrative, i.e. a creative reinterpretation of the Markan story. A similar view of the source question is found in Neyrey and Matera. In a study of Luke's sources in chapter 22, M. Soards concludes that Luke depends strongly on Mark but also blends in oral tradition and freely composed material; see M. Soards, *The Passion According to Luke*; J. Fitzmyer holds a similar view in his commentary.

proclamation of the Passion of Jesus takes on special hues.

Pinning down the circumstances of Luke's community is not an easy task. While certainly not always in agreement, biblical scholarship has been able to be more specific about Mark and Matthew on this score.[9] In Luke's case few possible geographical locations have been agreed upon, but there have been attempts to profile the circumstances of Luke's community.[10] Luke tracks the worldwide spread of the Gospel, originating in Israel through the ministry of Jesus and exploding out into the world through the Spirit-driven ministries of the apostles and Paul. This capital interest suggests that Luke's community was one in which the universal mission of the church—with the glories and problems it entailed—was a live issue. Luke gives attention to both ends of that mission: its foundation in the faith of Israel and its turbulent extension into the Gentile world in the person of Paul and the other early missionaries. While Luke may write for Gentiles, he shows great reverence for Judaism and its Law, and the lines of his story trace the origin of the Gospel from Jerusalem, the center of Jewish hopes.

The influence of Greco-Roman rhetoric on Luke (such as the stereotyped dedication to Theophilus in Luke 1:1-4 or the speeches found in Acts) and his efforts to tie the history of Jesus and the early community to the ongoing history of the Roman Empire (see, for example, 2:1; 3:1, etc.) indicate that Luke was thoroughly rooted in the Gentile world and conscious of the Roman political umbrella that dominated

[9]A number of recent interpreters argue for the traditional Roman setting of Mark's Gospel; see the discussion in D. Senior, "'With Swords and Clubs...' The Setting of Mark's Community and his Critique of Abusive Power," *Biblical Theology Bulletin* 17 (1987) 10-20; An Antioch setting for Matthew's Gospel is argued by J. Meier in R. Brown and J. Meier, *Antioch and Rome: New Testament Cradles of Catholic Christianity* (New York: Paulist, 1983).

[10]J. Fitzmyer despairs of naming any specific location but is firm about a post-70 dating for Luke-Acts; see J. Fitzmyer, *The Gospel According to Luke I-IX* (Anchor Bible 28; New York: Doubleday, 1981) 53-57; for a discussion of the circumstances of Luke's readers, see E. LaVerdiere, "New Testament Communities in Transition: A Study of Matthew and Luke," *Theological Studies* 37 (1976) 586-87; R. Karris, "Missionary Communities: A New Paradigm for the Study of Luke-Acts," *Catholic Biblical Quarterly* 41 (1979) 80-97.

it. Some interpreters think that Luke was anxious to mediate between the fledgling Christian church and that social and political world. The repeated declarations of Jesus' innocence on the part of Pilate and Herod, for example, may be part of Luke's attempt to show that the Christian movement need not be feared by the Roman authorities.[11] While Luke's community was thoroughly immersed in the Roman world, the evangelist's efforts to placate that milieu should not be over-emphasized. As we will point out in the course of our study, a story that portrays Jesus in such prophetic tones and climaxes with the Passion could never be fully digestible to the Roman empire.[12]

Other aspects of Luke's church seem to be detectable between the lines of his two-volume narrative. The portrayal of Jesus as a prophet who meets rejection, and the harassment experienced by the Jerusalem apostles and Paul in the course of their mission, may indicate that Luke's community had met its own share of persecution. At the same time Luke's attention to the poor and repeated warnings about the corruption of wealth and the importance of giving alms (many of them in parables addressed to the rich) could indicate that in Luke's community economic differences were a cause of tension.[13] If the threat of persecution existed, then relationships between rich and poor in the community might be complicated further since wealthier members might be more

[11]See, for example, P. Walasky, *'And So We Came to Rome'" The Political Perspective of St. Luke* (Cambridge: Cambridge University Press, 1983), and his earlier article, "The Trial and Death of Jesus in the Gospel of Luke," *Journal of Biblical Literature* 94 (1975) 81-93; also R. O'Toole, "Luke's Position on Politics and Society in Luke-Acts," in R. Cassidy and P. Scharper (eds.), *Political Issues in Luke-Acts* (Maryknoll: Orbis, 1983) 1-17; K. Wengst, *Pax Romana and the Peace of Jesus Christ* (Philadelphia: Fortress, 1987) 89-105; R. Maddox, *The Purpose of Luke-Acts* (Studies of the New Testament and Its World; London: T & T Clark, 1982) 91-99.

[12]A more adversarial stance to political structures is detected by R. Cassidy, *Jesus, Politics, and Society: A Study of Luke's Gospel* (Maryknoll: Orbis, 1978), esp. pp. 77-86; see further his follow-up study of Acts, *Society and Politics in the Acts of the Apostles* (Maryknoll: Orbis, 1987).

[13]R. Karris, "Poor and Rich: The Lukan Sitz im Leben," in C. Talbert (ed.), *Perspectives on Luke-Acts* (Macon: Mercer University Press, 1978) 112-25.

cautious if membership in the community could involve losing what they possessed.

It was to such a community that Luke addresses his Gospel. Although he sets out to write an "orderly account" for Theophilus (1:3), the "order" Luke has in mind is not a strict chronological order but one shaped by his understanding of how God's plan of salvation, a plan grounded in the history of Israel and come to fruition in the life of Jesus, had now moved under the guidance of the Spirit out into the Gentile world. Through the dynamic power of that story and the inspiration of its content, "Theophilus" (and the many Christians of his community who stood behind this audience of one) would come to know the full "truth" of the faith he had been given (1:4).

The distinctive perspective which informs Luke's account—what can be called his "theology"—is another reason for the quickening interest in this Gospel in recent scholarship. For a long time Luke's presentation of the death of Jesus was considered to be without much theological weight. The Passion was a stage through which Jesus passed on to the more important salvific events of Resurrection and Ascension. The story of Acts seemed to throw the weight of Luke's theological interest more towards the post-Easter period where the power of the Spirit sent by the Risen Christ created the community of faith and powered its mission to the world. Jesus' death was an eloquent example of suffering born faithfully, but little more.[14]

But recent studies of Luke's Gospel have not been content with this assessement.[15] No one would deny the importance of resurrection in Luke or the evangelist's focus on the Spirit's activity in the church. But Luke also grounded the victory of Easter in the death of Jesus. While he may not use atonement language, there are other important ways in which Luke

[14]This view is held by H. Conzelmann, *The Theology of Saint Luke* (London: Faber & Faber, 1960).

[15]This point is expressly taken up by J. Neyrey in his study of Lukan soteriology; see, *The Passion According to Luke*, esp., 156-92; also J. Fitzmyer, *The Gospel According to Luke I—IX*, pp. 219-27.

expresses the salvific nature of Jesus' death on the cross. Our own study of Luke's theology of the Passion will illustrate this in detail.

A final word about the approach taken in this book. The same format will be used as in the previous volumes of this series. *Part I.* Since the Passion story comes at the climax of the Gospel narrative and at the hinge point between the Gospel and Acts, we will first trace the way Luke prepares the reader for the Passion story within the body of the Gospel. What is accentuated in all of the Gospels is, if anything, more emphatically stated in Luke: The Passion of Jesus does not come as a rude surprise within the Gospel drama but is the outcome of challenges and threats orchestrated from the beginning of Jesus' mission. In *Part II* we will work our way through the entire Passion narrative of Luke 22 and 23, noting the evangelist's manner of retelling this foundational story. *Part III* will summarize the motifs of Luke's Passion story, relating them to the overall message of his Gospel and Acts, and suggesting ways that this theology may speak to us today.

The intended goal dictates the kind of methods to be used in analyzing Luke's Passion story. This study is not meant to be a demonstration of a single method of biblical exegesis, so no apology is offered for using an array of techniques, hopefully each used with integrity and understanding.[16] The primary interest of this study is Luke's intended message. While direct access to any author's intentions is impossible, a close reading of the Gospel, with its recurring patterns and emphases, its reinterpretations of Mark and Q, and its overall content and structure can yield a good sense of what Luke intended to communicate to his readers and, to some degree at least, what may have been the circumstances that shaped such a message. This is the goal of redaction criticism and the major goal of this book. Also useful are some methods of rhetorical or narrative criticism which highlight the literary dynamics of Luke's work and the ways in which they interact

---

[16]A helpful description of recently developed biblical methods can be found in T. Keegan, *Interpreting the Bible* (New York: Paulist, 1985).

with the reader. Although historical questions connected with the Passion of Jesus are fascinating, they are not the focus of this work.[17] Nor am I directly interested in the question of Luke's sources. Both issues will be touched on from time to time but only lightly.

As this volume draws to completion, I want to thank Ann Maloney, O.P. for her usual reliable and cheerful service in typing the various versions of the manuscript, and Marylyn Welter, O.S.F. for preparing the indexes.

[17]My assumption is that Luke has little historical information beyond that present in the account of his major source, Mark.

PART I
PREPARATION FOR THE DEATH OF JESUS

Luke begins his story of Jesus fully conscious of its endpoint, death and victory in Jerusalem. Death comes as no surprise for Jesus but as part of his God-given mission, a fearful yet inevitable climax to a prophetic destiny. The purpose of this chapter is to indicate some of the ways Luke prepares the reader for the death of Jesus.

The Framework of Luke's Story

The Gospel of Luke and its follow-through in Acts are narratives that carry the reader the entire span of Jesus' mission. Its general outline can be quickly traced. After a formal prologue explaining the purpose of his work (1:1-4), Luke opens his narrative with the birth of the Messiah in Bethlehem and his first appearance in the Jerusalem temple, a portent of things to come (1:5-2:52). The prelude for Jesus' ministry continues in the desert where the adult John and Jesus meet once more at the baptism and where Jesus first struggles with the power of evil (3:1-4:13). The explosive beginning of Jesus' public ministry is set by Luke in Nazareth and continues in healings and teaching throughout Galilee (4:14-9:50). Midway through the narrative there is a dramatic turn where Jesus sets his face toward Jerusalem and begins a purposeful journey which leads back to Jerusalem and, ultimately, through opposition and death, back to God (9:51-

19:27). Triumphant entry into the Holy City triggers a wave of opposition from the enemies of Jesus and leads to his final teaching on the destiny of the community (19:28-21:28). With the opposition intent on destroying Jesus and the moment of his mission of salvation about to be fulfilled, the Passion story now unfolds (22:1-23:56). The Gospel account ends with the triumph of the resurrection and Jesus' parting promise to send the Spirit upon the community he leaves behind (23:57-24:53).

The Acts of the Apostles picks up the narrative in describing the Spirit-filled community's birth at Pentecost (Acts 1:1-2:42), its unstoppable ministry in Jerusalem (2:43-8:3), and its gradually widening horizon as the Gospel radiates out from Jerusalem to reach Samaritans, and even Greeks in Antioch (8:4-9:43). The Spirit-directed acceptance of Cornelius, a Gentile soldier of Caesarea Maritima, into the community at the hands of Peter is a decisive turning point (10:1-11:18). The figure of Paul—once the persecutor and now a disciple— begins to loom larger. After the council in Jerusalem mediates between the Jewish and the Gentile missions (11:19-15:35), Paul's journeys out into the Mediterranean world and his own experiences of rejection and suffering dominate the rest of the story until the gospel reaches Rome (15:36-28:31).

Against the backdrop of this familiar story Luke prepares for the death of Jesus in the Gospel and demonstrates its life-giving impact upon the church within the account of Acts. Tracing that preparation in the Gospel and some of its follow-through in Acts will help us read Luke's Passion story with greater understanding.

Prelude at Nazareth

The inauguration of Jesus' public ministry in the synagogue of Nazareth, a scene unique to Luke's Gospel (4:16-30), can be considered the entire Gospel in miniature. Many of the major motifs of Luke's account—including his theology of the death of Jesus—are sounded in this overture to the public ministry of Jesus.

Warnings of deadly conflict could be detected earlier in the Gospel, at the very beginning of Jesus' life. Simeon's prophecy over the child had warned that the Messiah was "set for the fall and rising of many in Israel, and for a sign that is spoken against" (2:34). Mary's hymn praising God for pulling down the mighty from their thrones and sending the rich away hungry (1:52-53), and Zechariah's hopes for deliverance from the enemy and "from the hand of all who hate us" (1:71), could also be read, if obliquely, as early warning signs of deadly conflict to come. The signs could also be read in the fate of John the Baptist, the prophetic figure whom Luke presents in tandem with Jesus from the moment of their conception. John's preaching of the gospel and fearless confrontation with Herod lead to imprisonment (which Luke spells out much more clearly than either Mark or Matthew, see 3:18-20). No subtlety is needed to surmise that Jesus' preaching of the Gospel might also exact the same cost. Even more ominous is Luke's conclusion to the temptation scene. After exhausting every attempt to subvert Jesus' mission, Satan leaves him "until an opportune time" (4:13). That "opportune time" comes, the reader is to discover, with the Passion.

But in Luke's account these references to the impending death of Jesus are distant tollings of the bell. At Nazareth, the inevitable connection of death and opposition with the mission of Jesus breaks into the open. It is one of Luke's most powerful scenes and compressed into it are major motifs that will run throughout the Gospel.[1]

Luke skillfully sets the stage. It is introduced by the report of Jesus' entry into Galilee "in the power of the Spirit" (4:14); his teaching in the synagogues is received favorably by all (4:15). The reader is set for a description of just such a triumph within Jesus' own home community. The opening segments of the scene move on this level. Jesus takes his place in the synagogue on the Sabbath and is given the book of Isaiah to read. He unrolls the scroll to Isaiah 61 and reads

---

[1] On the role of this scene in Luke's overall theology, see D. Tiede, *Prophecy and History in Luke-Acts* (Philadelphia: Fortress, 1980), esp., 19-64.

a passage that will be programmatic for the entire messianic mission of Jesus:

> "The Spirit of the Lord is upon me, because he has anointed me to preach good news to the poor. He has sent me to proclaim release to the captives and recovering of sight to the blind, to set at liberty those who are oppressed, to proclaim the acceptable year of the Lord."[2]

Luke focuses our attention on the response that follows, that of Jesus and the people of Nazareth. Jesus gives the scroll back to the attendant, sits down, and, Luke notes, "the eyes of all in the synagogue were fixed on him" (4:20). Jesus' first words declare that the message of liberation proclaimed by Isaiah finds its ultimate meaning in his own messianic mission: "Today this scripture has been fulfilled in your hearing" (4:21). This declaration, too, is well received by the people of Nazareth ("All spoke well of him, and wondered at the gracious words which proceeded out of his mouth"). But their murmur of approval betrays a narrowness of perspective, a perspective that Jesus will quickly challenge: "Is not this Joseph's son?" (4:22).

But Jesus shatters the harmony of this scene. He cites a proverb—"Physician, heal yourself"—which spotlights the crimped horizons of the Nazarenes. They want to see the display of power Jesus had unleashed in other places confined to their own circle. Jesus' response is hardly reassuring; he recalls the ministries of Elijah and Elisha— the great prophetic figures of Israel's history. Elijah was called to deliver a woman of Sidon; Elisha, to cure a Syrian leper. Neither prophet was confined to Israel. The expansive vision of Jesus, moving beyond the boundaries of Israel, is too much for the hometown congregation: "all in the synagogue were filled with wrath" (4:28). Their hostility boils over and they drive Jesus out of his own city and attempt to kill him by casting him over the brow of a hill. But it is not yet the opportune

---

[2]The actual text quoted by Luke is a composite of Isaiah 61:1-2 and 58:6.

time and Jesus passes through their midst and goes his way (4:30).

It is not difficult to see why this scene could be considered a preview of Luke's Gospel as a whole. Jesus' ministry of salvation which is to be proclaimed to the world meets with misunderstanding and rejection. He is threatened with death but is not overcome by it, going his own way as he is destined. The ministry, Passion and resurrection of Jesus are all subtlely anticipated in this inaugural text.

Leads to the Passion

The specific motifs found in this passage also alert us to the several ways in which Luke prepares for the Passion within the body of his Gospel and it is these we will now chart.

THE CHALLENGE OF JUSTICE

The bold words of Isaiah quoted in the Nazareth passage—good news to the poor, release of captives, sight for the blind, liberty for the oppressed, the proclamation of the Jubilee year of reconciliation and renewal—reveal the heart of Jesus' ministry as described by Luke. These actions typify what it means to proclaim the advent of God's rule. The God of justice would establish justice, especially for those most deprived of it: the poor, the disabled, the alienated, the oppressed. Proclaiming the coming of God's Kingdom and bringing it about in his actions define Jesus' mission: "I must preach the good news of the kingdom of God ... for I was sent for this purpose" (4:43). Jesus' preaching in the synagogue of Nazareth illustrates what the advent of the Kingdom would mean.[3]

---

[3]On this important New Testament metaphor, see D. Senior, "Reign of God," in J. Komonchak, M. Collins, D. Lane (eds.), *The New Dictionary of Theology* (Wilmington: Michael Glazier, 1987) 851-61.

These same acts of salvation are, paradoxically, the cause of much of the opposition that mounts against Jesus. Because God's justice challenges inequity and false values, it is fiercely resisted. This point is made by Jesus himself when responding to the disciples of John the Baptist who came to investigate Jesus' messianic credentials:

> Go and tell John what you have seen and heard: the blind receive their sight, the lame walk, lepers are cleansed, and the deaf hear, the dead are raised up, the poor have the good news preached to them. And blessed is the one who takes no offense at me. (7:22-23)

In Luke's account, the Pharisees and other Jewish leaders become the embodiment of those who "take offense" because their lives and values run counter to that of the Kingdom of God.[4] Luke frames that judgement in Jesus' own words: "But woe to you Pharisees! for you tithe mint and rue and every herb and neglect justice and the love of God; these you ought to have done, without neglecting the others" (11:42). Therefore they become the resistance to Jesus. As the Gospel unfolds the reader soon realizes that Jesus' ministry is provoking deadly hostility; the way to the Passion has begun.

Examples abound. Forgiving the sins of the paralytic stirs the opposition of the Scribes and Pharisees at Jesus' claim to such authority (5:21). Jesus' meal with tax collectors and sinners in the house of Levi draws a murmur of scandal from these same leaders (5:30). The healing of man with a withered hand on the Sabbath kindles their rage and the first stirrings of a plot to destroy him (6:6-11). Simon the Pharisee is shocked that Jesus would accept the bold tenderness offered by a sinful woman (7:39). Jesus' liberation of those controlled by evil spirits is misinterpreted by the leaders as an act of solidarity with Satan (11:15). His Sabbath healing of the woman bent double meets the disapproval of the synagogue manager (13:14). Herod seeks to kill him, presuma-

---

[4]On the various opponents of Jesus in Luke's Gospel, see J. Tyson, *The Death of Jesus*, 47-83.

bly because of the cures and exorcisms Jesus will not cease doing (13:31-32). While dining on the Sabbath at the house of a powerful Pharisee ruler, Jesus cures a man with dropsy and earns the silent, hostile rage of his hosts (14:1-6). Constant kinship with tax collectors and sinners fuels the Pharisees' opposition (15:1-2). His opponents scoff at his warnings on the lure of wealth and the necessity of sharing possessions (16:14). His bold purification of the Temple galvanizes the opposition and they conspire to kill him (19:45-47). His sharp exchanges with the leaders while teaching in the Temple provoke them to the point of wanting to seize him on the spot—only fear of the crowds restraining them and making them content to lie in wait to trap him (20:19-20).

Luke draws a direct line between the proclamation of the Kingdom of God and the cross. The image of the servant Jesus in the last supper scene is filled out in the life-giving ministry of Jesus in the Gospel (see 22:27). In pouring out his energy and compassion on behalf of the poor and the sick, Jesus the servant prepared for his own death.

BREAKING THE BOUNDARIES

The salvation proclaimed by Jesus breaks beyond the boundaries of Israel and seeps out into the world. Not just the people of Israel, but Gentiles, too, would experience the salvation proclaimed by Jesus. This is another motif, strongly present in the Nazareth scene and closely related to the theme of justice, which helps prepare the reader for the Passion of Jesus in Luke.

Luke announces that theme when reflecting on the ministry of John the Baptist; he quotes from Isaiah 40:5:

> "Every valley shall be filled, and every mountain and hill shall be made straight, and the rough ways shall be made smooth; and *all flesh shall see the salvation of God.*"

That same quotation is alluded to at the conclusion of Acts, when Paul is in Rome and vows to continue preaching the "kingdom of God and teaching about the Lord Jesus" (Acts 28:30) to the Gentiles: "Let it be known to you then that this *salvation of God* has been sent to the Gentiles; they will listen." (Acts 27:28).

The centrifugal thrust of God's salvation—grounded in the history of Israel, embodied in the person and ministry of Jesus, and through the power of the Spirit breaking out to the whole world—is a fundamental current running through Luke's entire two volume work.[5] It is clearly present in the inaugural scene at Nazareth where Jesus declares to his hometown congregation that, in the manner of Elijah and Elisha who crossed boundaries into Sidon and Syria, his ministry would not be confined "to his own homeland" (4:23). That challenge ignites the congregation's fury, and the combustion of that first encounter would happen again in the course of Jesus' ministry, leading ultimately to the cross itself. Reaching beyond the perimeters of any community can be dangerous. To have dealings with an "outsider" or even to acknowledge their presence at the perimeter can disturb a well-defined community. To bring "outsiders" in and treat them on an equal basis can be revolutionary.

The early Christian community knew these dynamics well as it struggled to define itself in the context of the Greco-Roman world. The sense of heritage and identity felt by Jewish Christians could be threatened by the infusion of Gentile converts. And for all, Jew and Gentile, the outward thrust of the Gospel could clash with the need for community cohesiveness in the face of the dominant culture and values of the world. Some of the stories about Jesus' boundary-breaking ministry reflect this same kind of tension.

Jesus' association with tax collectors and sinners, noted several times in the Gospel of Luke, is one important example. Tax collectors, as collaborators with the Gentile over-

<hr/>

[5]On the Gentile mission in Luke-Acts, see J. Dupont, *The Salvation of the Gentiles: Studies in the Acts of the Apostles* (Mahwah: Paulist, 1979); S.G. Wilson, *The Gentiles and the Gentile Mission in Luke-Acts* (Cambridge: Cambridge University Press, 1973); D. Senior & C. Stuhlmueller, *The Biblical Foundations for Mission* (Maryknoll: Orbis, 1983) 255-79.

lords of the people, were socially repugnant and ritually impure. "Sinners"—presumably a grouping of those who habitually violated the law—were religiously unacceptable. These social and religious pariahs evidently fell into the "unclean" zone and were marginalized members of the community of the redeemed.[6] For a public person such as Jesus to associate with them, and much worse, to eat with them, was an affront and a threat because it challenged the leaders' definition of who belonged within the community of Israel.

Luke's account is filled with examples of boundary breaking on Jesus' part. Inviting Levi the tax collector into his company of disciples (5:27-28) and then dining with him and a large group of fellow tax collectors lead to a "murmur" of opposition by the Pharisees (5:29-32). Jesus is clearly aware of his opponents' scandal: he plays back their hostile assessment when reflecting on the rejection experienced by John and himself: "For John the Baptist has come eating no bread and drinking no wine; and you say, 'He has a demon.' The Son of man has come eating and drinking; and you say, 'Behold, a glutton and a drunkard, a friend of tax collectors and sinners!'" (7:33-34).

That angry buzz is repeated in chapter 15, immediately prior to the three great mercy parables: "This man receives sinners and eats with them." (15:2). In a story found only in Luke, Jesus invites himself to dinner at Zaccheus' house, "a chief tax collector, and rich" (19:2), earning the same hostile response from the observers: "He has gone in to be the guest of a man who is a sinner" (19:7). Jesus' response to this criticism shows that Luke has the universal sweep of salvation in mind: "Today salvation has come to this house, since he also is a son of Abraham. For the Son of man came to seek and to save the lost" (19:9-10).

The widening horizon of salvation displayed in Jesus' association with tax collectors and sinners is also visible in his dealings with women and Gentiles. Luke clearly states that women were part of Jesus' company of disciples (see, for

---

[6]For the historical context see E.P. Sanders, *Jesus and Judaism* (Philadelphia: Fortress, 1985) 174-211.

example, 8:1-3). While Luke does not seem to deal directly
with the exclusion of women in his milieu, their more peri-
pheral role within Jewish and Greco-Roman society is an
assumed backdrop of his story.[7] The taboos of ritual purity
in the Jewish Law for touching a woman in public or as-
sociating with one who is sick further isolated them. Several
times in Luke, Jesus cuts through this thicket, often provoking the anger of the guardians of the boundaries. In
chapter 7, for instance, immediately after the saying cited
above about Jesus as "a friend of tax collectors and sinners"
(7:34), Luke inserts his special story (not found in the other
Gospels) about a feast at the house of Simon the Pharisee
(7:36-50). During the meal, a "woman of the city, who was a
sinner" breaks into the circle of the dinner guests and lavishes
bold acts of tenderness on Jesus, washing his feet with her
tears, anointing them with precious ointment, and wiping
them dry with her hair. The Pharisee host glares, thoroughly
scandalized. But Jesus, openly rejecting Simon's judgment,
accepts the woman's love and declares her sins forgiven because "she loved much" (7:47).

Later in Jesus' ministry, in another of Luke's special
stories, Jesus interrupts a synagogue Sabbath service to heal
a disabled woman (13:10-17). The intrusion infuriates the
synagogue manager who, oblivious to her cure, lashes out at
the woman: "There are six days on which work ought to be
done; come on those days and be healed, and not on the
sabbath day." (13:14). Once again Jesus' response reveals
that the spirit of inclusion is close to the surface of this story:
"Ought not this woman, a daughter of Abraham whom Satan
bound for eighteen years, be loosed from this bond on the
sabbath day?" (13:16). The "salvation of God" which Jesus
embodies cannot be denied by boundaries of gender or time
or religious propriety.

Another group beyond the boundaries was the Gentiles.
Here, too, Luke notes Jesus' open spirit. Unlike Matthew
and Mark who construct an extended journey of Jesus into

---

[7]For a survey of the historical background, see B. Witherington III, *Women in
the Ministry of Jesus* (Cambridge: Cambridge University Press, 1984).

Gentile territory, Luke has few incidents in the Gospel where Jesus deals directly with Gentiles.[8] In Luke's presentation, the Gentiles' first serious encounter with the message of salvation comes in Acts through the preaching of the Apostles and other missionaries. But this mission of the church is founded on the spirit of Jesus' own expansive mission, and Luke already points to the inclusion of Gentiles in the Gospel itself.

One actual encounter is the healing of the Roman Centurion's slave (7:1-10). In Luke's account (compare Matthew 8:5-13) this official is presented as a benefactor of the Jewish people at Capernaum; the elders of the village even recommend him to Jesus. But a note of discord comes at the end of the story. The faith of the Centurion amazes Jesus and he tells the crowds: "I tell you, not even in Israel have I found such faith" (7:9). Implicit here is a tragic theme that moves throughout Luke's two volume work: the rejection of Jesus and the Gospel by Israel are coupled, paradoxically, to their acceptance by the Gentiles.[9] That same note of discord is present in several of Jesus' sayings where rejection by Israel is contrasted with the openness of the Gentiles. The impenitent attitude of the Galilean cities of Chorazin and Bethsaida is unfavorably compared to that of Tyre and Sidon (10:13-14). The Queen of the South and people of Nineveh will fare better at the judgment than "this generation" (11:29-32). In another judgment text, those who reject Jesus are promised they will be "thrust out" of the kingdom of God, while Gentiles "will come from east and west, and from north and south, and sit at table in the kingdom of God" (13:28-29).

In all these examples, Jesus' boundary-breaking ministry to tax collectors and sinners, to women and Gentiles (and

[8]This is partly due to Luke's "great omission" of the material found in Mark 6:45-8:26 with its stories of Jesus' encounter with the Syro-Phoenician woman and the feeding on the Gentile side of the lake. In addition to the Centurion story, Jesus heals the Gadarene demoniac in Luke 8:26-30.

[9]This note is sounded at the very end of Acts when Paul experiences a mixed reception to his preaching from Jews at Rome (Acts 28:23-29). On this issue, see the balanced treatment of R. Maddox, *The Purpose of Luke-Acts*, 31-65.

one could extend the list to Samaritans and the sick and the poor) is linked with hostility and rejection on the part of the leaders of Israel. Jesus' mission of universal salvation would be costly, Luke warns us. Once again the evangelist prepares the reader for the approaching Passion.

THE REJECTED PROPHET

The Jesus who preaches in the synagogue of Nazareth is a Spirit-filled prophet. He invokes the text of Isaiah, "The Spirit of the Lord is upon me, because I have been anointed..." (4:18). And the models for his inclusive mission are the great prophetic figures, Elijah and Elisha (4:25-27). There is little doubt that Luke uses the mantle of prophecy as one of the important ways of understanding Jesus and his mission. The gift of the Spirit, one of the marks of prophetic power, is granted to Jesus and those associated with him. The spirit of prophecy floods the infancy story. Mary's conception of Jesus happens through the power of the Spirit (1:35). And the great Jewish characters of the infancy gospel— Elizabeth (1:41), Zechariah (1:67), Simeon (2:27)—are all moved to speak prophetically. Anna who recognizes Jesus as God's gift of redemption is described as a "prophetess" (2:36). The Spirit descends upon Jesus' himself at the Jordan (3:22), leads him into a victorious desert confrontation with Satan (4:1) and plunges him into his mission in Galilee (4:14). Jesus' acts of mercy, such as the raising of the widow's son at Naim, move the crowd to acclaim, "A great prophet has arisen among us, and God has visited his people!" (7:16-17).

But Luke is not content to portray Jesus' prophetic mission as one of unrepressed power. In the Hebrew Scriptures the prophetic vocation was also linked to rejection.[10] The prophet plays a painful role in God's relentless courtship of Israel.

---

[10]On this motif, see R. Dillon, "Easter Revelation and Mission Program in Luke 24:46-48," in D. Durken, *Sin, Salvation, and the Spirit* (Collegeville: Liturgical Press, 1979), 240-70, esp., 248-51, and his monograph, *From Eye-Witnesses to Ministers of the Word. Tradition and Composition in Luke 24* (Rome: Biblical Institute press, 1978).

The prophet's message of repentance is repeatedly rejected, and the life of the prophet threatened. The prophet is stung with the hostility of a people who refuse to change. But rejection and death are not the last words in this turbulent relationship: even in failure the prophet is the guarantee of God's abiding care for Israel.

Those elements are beautifully expressed in one of the Old Testament passages where this theme is present:

> "Nevertheless they were disobedient and rebelled against thee and cast thy law behind their back and killed thy prophets, who had warned them in order to turn them back to thee, and they committed great blasphemies. Therefore thou didst give them into the hand of their enemies, who made them suffer; and in the time of their suffering they cried to thee and thou didst hear them from heaven; and according to thy great mercies thou didst give them saviors who saved them from the hand of their enemies. But after they had rest they did evil again before thee, and thou didst abandon them to the hand of their enemies, so that they had dominion over them; yet when they turned and cried to thee thou didst hear from heaven, and many times thou didst deliver them according to thy mercies.... Many years thou didst bear with them, and didst warn them by thy Spirit through thy prophets; yet they would not give ear. Therefore thou didst give them into the hand of the peoples of the lands. Nevertheless in thy great mercies thou didst not make an end of them or forsake them; for thou art a gracious and merciful God." (Nehemiah 9:26-31).

The way Luke describes Jesus' reception at Nazareth shows that the evangelist is very conscious of this dimension of the prophetic vocation. Jesus quotes the ominous proverb: 'Truly, I say to you, no prophet is acceptable in his own country" (4:24). The murderous intent of the townspeople proves the saying true. Therefore right from the beginning of Jesus' ministry Luke warns the reader that Jesus will suffer the fate of the martyr-Prophets.

At key points along the course of his ministry, similar warnings are given. In the Sermon on the Plain Jesus instructs the disciples:

> "Blessed are you when people hate you, and when they exclude you and revile you, and cast out your name as evil, on account of the Son of man! Rejoice in that day, and leap for joy, for behold, your reward is great in heaven; for so their ancestors did to the prophets." (6:22-23).

Jesus blisters the lawyers ("who load people with burdens hard to bear") and pronounces a judgment over them, a judgment that is also a forshadowing of Jesus' death:

> "Woe to you! for you build the tombs of the prophets whom your fathers killed. So you are witnesses and consent to the deeds of your fathers; for they killed them, and you build their tombs. Therefore also the Wisdom of God said, 'I will send them prophets and apostles, some of whom they will kill and persecute,' that the blood of all the prophets, shed from the foundation of the world, may be required of this generation. . . ." (11:47-50).

No text is more explicit about all this than Jesus' challenge to Herod, a text special to Luke's Gospel. Pharisees warn Jesus that Herod Antipas, the ruler of Galilee during the adult life of Jesus, wanted to kill him.[11] The threat is sharply turned back by Jesus:

> "Go and tell that fox, 'Behold, I cast out demons and perform cures today and tomorrow, and the third day I finish my course. Nevertheless I must go on my way today and tomorrow and the day following; for it cannot be that a prophet should perish away from Jerusalem." (13:32-33)

---

[11]Herod will reappear in the Passion story; see below Lk 23:6-12.

Luke couples to this a poignant lament over Jerusalem in which Jesus' own rejection and death in the Holy City are foretold:

> "O Jerusalem, Jerusalem, killing the prophets and stoning those who are sent to you! How often would I have gathered your children together as a hen gathers her brood under her wings, and you would not! Behold, your house is forsaken. And I tell you, you will not see me until you say, 'Blessed is he who comes in the name of the Lord!'" (13:34-35).

The fate of all those prophetic forbearers, rejected because of their message of repentance, would fall upon Jesus. Another Jerusalem lament brings the prophet Jesus to the brink of the Passion. As he draws near the city at the end of his long journey from Galilee, the sight of it causes Jesus to weep: "Would that even today you knew the things that make for peace! But now they are hid from your eyes...." (19:41).

But this poignant last plea is not heard; as Jesus enters Jerusalem and teaches in its temple, Luke notes that "the chief priests and the scribes and the principal men of the people sought to destroy him" (19:47). As in the case of Jesus' commitment to justice and his proclamation of universal salvation, his prophetic mission stirs implacable forces of opposition and leads the gospel story to the cross.

THE TEST OF EVIL

The Gospel of Luke is filled with the kind of conflict that erupted in the synagogue of Nazareth. As we have noted throughout this chapter, the mission of Jesus is continually met with opposition, usually from the leaders, especially the Pharisees in the body of the Gospel, and the chief priests once the story moves into Jerusalem.[12] Jesus is not a passive

---

[12]On the role of conflict in Luke, see J. Tyson, *The Death of Jesus in Luke-Acts*, 48-83.

victim of this violence; he actively challenges his opponents and is not afraid of the conflict that results. He characterizes his own mission as a "fire" he longed to cast upon the earth (12:49); his zeal was not to bring flaccid peace, but "division" (12:51-53). The enemies of Jesus are one dimensional characters, representing the antithesis of the values proclaimed by Jesus. Thus they protest his forgiveness of sins (5:17-26), take offense at his healings, and are portrayed as full of greed and hypocrisy, smug in their self-righteousness. Their fury finally boils over and they plot to destroy Jesus; eventually they effect his arrest and his death.

But Luke's Gospel is not content to see the drama of Jesus' mission played out only on a human stage. The cross is not simply the by-product of human weakness and sin. There is a deeper, even more foreboding, conflict that runs throughout Luke's Gospel. The Passion of Jesus is part of a cosmic drama in which ultimate goodness and ultimate evil struggle for victory.[13]

Luke makes that clear in the first conflict story of the Gospel, the test in the desert (4:1-13). The placement of the story immediately after the baptism and the genealogy (tracing Jesus' lineage back to Adam, back to God) gives it heightened force as the very first act of the Spirit-filled Messiah. The desert setting and the forty day duration (4:2) evoke the wilderness period of Israel itself, when it was first formed as a people and was tested for its commitment to Yahweh. Now Jesus, the embodiment of Israel's hopes, would endure that same desert test.

Three times Satan attempts to pervert Jesus' mission (the last, in Jerusalem where Jesus' own ministry would end) but each time his lure is thrust aside. Defeated, the prince of evil leaves Jesus, but, the Gospel notes, only "until an opportune time" (4:13). The evangelist clearly sees the Passion itself as the final proving ground for Jesus' messianic mission. At the beginning of the Passion story, Satan "enter(s) into Judas

---

[13]See J. Neyrey, *The Passion According to Luke*, 31-33 for an excellent summary of the role of Satan in Luke's Gospel.

called Iscariot" (22:3) and the events leading to Jesus' death begin their fateful sequence.[14]

But conflict with the demonic is not confined to the Passion story. Throughout the Gospel Luke alerts the reader to the cosmic dimension of Jesus' struggle with evil and thereby prepares for another important aspect of the Passion. The exorcism stories are one arena in which that struggle is carried out. In harmony with most of the New Testament, Luke sees evil at the root of human pain.[15] It is not a matter of the sick or disabled being by necessity morally responsible for their conditions (a position explicitly rejected in Luke's Gospel, see 13:1-5). Rather, Satan, as the personification of evil, was seen to hold humanity captive, a demonic oppressive force, de-humanizing its prisoners, robbing them of their freedom and human dignity. The tyranny of this chronic, pervasive evil manifested itself in human afflictions that the biblical peoples feared and for which they could find no remedy: mental illness, mysterious, unpredictable forms of sickness.

Therefore some of Jesus' healings become a battleground. Only after violent struggle is the demoniac released from his torment in the synagogue of Capernaum (4:31-37). Jesus' liberation of the possessed man living among the tombs in the land of the Gerasenes is accompanied with shouts and fierce struggle, as demons infest a herd of swine and return to the "abyss" of the sea, a traditional abode of evil spirits (8:26-39).[16] A powerful evil spirit afflicts a young boy, convulsing and "shattering" him, a demon so strong only Jesus can drive him out (9:37-43). It is Satan who holds bound the

[14]Luke also refers to Jesus' impending death as a "trial," the same key Greek word *peirasmos* used in the temptation story; see below 22:28, 40, 46.

[15]On this question see K. Seybold & U. Mueller, *Sickness & Healing* (Nashville: Abingdon, 1981); P. Borgen, "Miracles of Healing in the New Testament: Some Observations," *Studia Theologica* 35 (1981) 91-106; for a sociological perspective on uncleanness associated with sickness, see B. Malina, *The New Testament World: Insights from Cultural Anthropology* (Atlanta: John Knox, 1981), 122-52.

[16]On the often hostile connotation of the sea in biblical literature, see J.P. Heil, *Jesus Walking On the Sea: Meaning and Functions of Matt 14:22-23, Mark 6:45-52 and John 6:15b-21* (Rome: Biblical Institute, 1981).

woman bent double; Jesus triumphantly releases this "daughter of Abraham" from her oppression (13:10-17).

Struggles with the elements of nature reinforce the cosmic proportions of the conflict in which Jesus is engaged. As noted above, the "sea" evoked images of chaos for biblical peoples; it was the abode of threatening spirits. Jesus first encounters the disciples at the sea (5:1-11). They have struggled all night and gained nothing. With a single word Jesus directs them to an abundant catch. Although open conflict with the demonic is not mentioned here, its placement between stories of exorcism and healing suggest that this backdrop is not absent from Luke's perspective.[17] That struggle breaks into the open in the story of the storm at sea (8:22-25). Angry waves threatened to engulf the disciples like a vengeful demon. But Jesus "silences" (*epetimēsen*) the wind and the raging sea. The Greek word used here is the same forceful language used in the exorcism stories (see 4:35, 8:30, 9:42). The demonic sea is tamed and the disciples are rescued by the "Master" (the title, *epistata*, used for Jesus in this story reflects the power he exercises over the demonic forces).

Summaries of Jesus' activity indicate that, from Luke's perspective, these therapeutic combats with the demonic were an integral part of Jesus' messianic mission (see 4:40-41; 6:18; 8:2). Even what seem to be some straightforward healing stories edge towards being exorcisms: the "fever" that grips Simon's mother-in-law is "silenced" (*epetimēsen*) as if it were a demon and she is freed to "serve" as Jesus served (4:39).[18]

In fact all strands of conflict seem to coalesce around Jesus' struggle with the demonic: the exorcisms and even the healings as struggles with human pain whose origin is ultimately judged as a demonic attack on the beauty of human life; the arbitrary threat of nature's anger in the unyielding

---

[17]See J. Tyson, *The Death of Jesus in Luke-Acts*, 60. Note that later the disciples themselves will be caught up in Jesus' struggle with the demonic, as the seventy report on their return from mission (10:17).

[18]Note the use of the key word *diakonein* (to "serve") here, as in 22:27 where Jesus characterizes his entire ministry in terms of table serving.

harvest of the sea and the rage of the storm; the aggressive hostility of Jesus' opponents.[19]

The story of Judas' apostasy will show that not even Jesus' disciples are exempt from being used as agents of the demon. Even if the other disciples should escape radical failure, they, too, would be drawn into combat with ultimate evil. The Gospel gives a preview of this in the experience of the seventy disciples sent out on mission. They return exuberant, "Lord even the demons are subject to us in your name!" (10:17). Their first triumph triggers a prophetic vision in Jesus which validates their joy but tempers it at the same time:

> "I saw Satan fall like lightning from heaven. Behold, I have given you authority to tread upon serpents and scorpions, and over all the power of the enemy; and nothing shall hurt you. Nevertheless do not rejoice in this, that the spirits are subject to you; but rejoice that your names are written in heaven" (10:18-20)

The Passion illustrates that the community's struggle with evil should not be underestimated; only the power of God could determine the outcome.

THE DESTINY OF THE CHRIST: JESUS' JOURNEY TO GOD

Jesus' encounter with evil is not the deepest current that flows beneath the story line of Luke. Another cosmic motif, most fundamental of all, draws the reader through the Gospel toward the Passion: The Christ "must" meet death because it is God's will that the Christ enter into his glory. This major motif also has echoes in the inaugural scene at Nazareth. The Jesus who announces a mission of expansive justice and experiences lethal opposition because of it, is a Jesus whose

---

[19]See the parable of the wandering demon which returns to its former house with seven other spirits more evil than itself (11:24-26)—a story directed at those who had accused Jesus of working in league wth Beelzebul the prince of demons (11:15).

words and actions "fulfill" the Scriptures. Fidelity to God's will leads to the "necessity" of the cross.

That "divine necessity" is proclaimed in each of the resurrection stories at the end of the Gospel, by the two heavenly messengers at the tomb (24:7), by the Risen Christ himself as he dispels the gloom of the two disciples on the way to Emmaus (24:26-27), and when he appears to all of the community in Jerusalem (24:46). It is also repeated in several of the speeches in the Acts of the Apostles.[20] The suffering of Jesus was not a tragic waste, nor mere endurance. Mysteriously, it fulfilled the vocation of the messiah revealed cumulatively in the Scriptures and in the destiny of the prophets.[21]

In the course of the Gospel, reference to the "must" of Jesus' Passion is a fundamental motif that carries the reader through the narrative to the Passion story. In 9:22, Jesus responds to Peter's confession of him as "the Christ of God" with a solemn prophetic declaration: "The Son of man must suffer many things, and be rejected by the elders and chief priests and scribes, and be killed, and on the third day be raised." That prophecy is emphatically repeated in 9:44: "Let these words sink into your ears; for the Son of man is to be delivered into the hands of men." Later he instructs his disciples on the signs of the end time: "For as the lightning flashes and lights up the sky from one side to the other, so will the Son of man be in his day. But first he must suffer many things and be rejected by this generation" (17:24-25).

These declarations do not float free in Luke's Gospel; they are enveloped in a fateful journey that carries Jesus from Galilee to Jerusalem, from the region where his mission of the Kingdom is displayed with breathtaking power, to that city where the Temple of God shimmered on Mount Sion and where prophets were killed. Casting the ministry of Jesus into the potent framework of a journey was already the genius of Mark's Gospel.[22] But Luke will develop that fateful

[20]Acts 1:16; 2:23; 4:28; 13:26-37; 17:3; On this motif, see J. Fitzmyer, *The Gospel According to Luke I-IX*, 179-91.

[21]See D. Tiede, *Prophecy and History in Luke-Acts*, esp., 97-125.

[22]See D. Senior, *The Passion of Jesus in the Gospel of Mark*, 28-35.

journey of Jesus into a memorable symbol of his dedication to the will of God.

Intimations of that are found already in the Infancy Gospel. The boy Jesus travels from Galilee to Jerusalem with his parents and, to their consternation, will not leave because he "must be in (his) Father's house" (2:49). When the hostile synagogue congregation of Nazareth attempts to kill him he passes through their midst and travels on his way (4:30). At the beginning of his pubic ministry, Jesus will not let himself be restrained by the crowds because "he must preach the good news of the kingdom of God to the other cities also; for I was sent for this purpose" (4:43).

Midway through the Gospel Luke explicitly introduces the journey motif:

> "When the days drew near for him to be received up, he set his face to go to Jerusalem. And he sent messengers ahead of him, who went and entered a village of the Samaritans, to make ready for him; but the people would not receive him, because his face was set toward Jerusalem" (9:51-52).

This passage has the marks of Luke's careful work. It is the first mention of Jerusalem as the endpoint of Jesus' mission. Luke stresses Jesus' determination to take that journey: "he set (literally, "stiffened") his face." A moment of crucial time was at hand: the days of his *analēmpsis*, his "being-taken-up" were "filled up" (*symplērousthai*). Each word is drenched with meaning. Reference to "being-taken-up" shows that the endpoint of this Journey is not just the city of Jerusalem but Jesus' return to God. Only in Luke's account does the ascension of Jesus, his glorious return to God, play such a crucial role (see Luke 24:51-53; Acts 1:1-11, 22).[23] Throughout the Gospel the reader is being forewarned that such a journey must first pass through the experience of death.

But this is not to be one death among many. The return of Jesus to God comes at the "filling up" of the time. Luke

[23]See J. Fitzmyer, "The Ascension of Christ and Pentecost," *Theological Studies* 45 (1984) 409-40.

presents Jesus as the fulfillment of Israel's hopes, the embodiment of God's faithful promises to the people. Jesus himself had preached to the people of Nazareth: "Today this scripture has been fulfilled in your hearing" (Luke 4:21, the word for "fulfilled," *peplērōtai*, is the same root word as in 9:51). The message of liberation announced in Isaiah's text comes to life in the ministry of Jesus; the time of salvation which Israel longed for was now at hand. As the determined start of the journey towards Jerusalem implies and as the Passion story will make clear, the fulfillment of that mission comes as Jesus passes through death and enters his glory.

Luke follows through on this journey motif in the rest of the Gospel. Occasional references to journeying are inserted along the way (see, 9:56-57; 10:38; 13:31, 33; 17:11; 19:28). And the goal of Jerusalem is repeated (see 13:22, 33-34; 17:11; 18:31; 19:11, 28). But Luke does not present Jesus as a man in perpetual motion. He inserts into this long expanse of the Gospel (9:51-19:41) many of Jesus' parables and discourses. The most important instructions on discipleship are also found here. Thus at the same time Jesus is "on the road" the narrative seems curiously static. In effect, Luke wants the journey to encompass the most demanding of Jesus' teachings. With Jerusalem and the cross in view the disciples learn what it means to follow Jesus. The faithful God of mercy and justice beckons to Jesus and to all who would walk with him.[24] But as the story unfolds the readers discover that fidelity to this way leads to opposition, rejection, even death itself. It is here that the "must" of Jesus' death is revealed; not a "must" of faceless destiny or unthinking fanatical devotion, but a "must" that comes from fidelity to a divine vocation to take up one's cross and to give one's life, no matter what the cost.[25]

---

[24]Luke himself uses this image for discipleship; see for example Acts 2:21-22 when the criteria for choosing a replacement for Judas are laid down by Peter. An apostle must be one of those "who have accompanied us during all the time that the Lord Jesus went in and out among us, beginning from the baptism of John until the day when he was taken up from us."

[25]For further discussion of this important part of Luke's christology, see Part III, pp. 173-77.

Jesus' fidelity to God's plan of salvation is the ultimate key to all of the ways Luke prepares the reader for the Passion. Proclamation of justice is the heartbeat of God's salvation and opposition to it turns the story of Jesus toward death. The expansive horizon of that salvation strains against the narrow expectations of the leaders of Israel and once again the cross looms. The recurring pattern of love offered and love rejected found in the history of the prophets insures the Passion for the prophet Jesus. And lurking beneath and beyond all of this resistance to God's salvation stands ultimate evil—pervasive, chronic, aggressive, using its final weapon of death to strike at the savior. No one can read Luke's Gospel and not become aware that it leads to the story of death and victory in Jerusalem. The motifs traced throughout the Gospel now merge and find their climax in the final chapter of Jesus' mission of salvation. To that Passion story we now turn.

PART II
THE PASSION OF JESUS

Having prepared the reader, Luke now begins his account of the Passion. His debt to Mark for most of his material is clear, but Luke puts his own characteristic stamp on the narrative.

Overview of Luke's Passion Narrative

Luke's Passion narrative moves swiftly from the conspiracy of the leaders to the burial of Jesus' crucified body. It begins with a prelude that quickly envelops the reader in the Passion drama, as the plot to destroy Jesus takes shape (22:1-6). A major scene for Luke is the final passover. It begins with the disciples' preparation of the meal (22:7-13) and then the passover celebration itself, a scene Luke enriches with a final discourse of Jesus (22:14-38). The mood darkens as Jesus and his disciples move to the Mount of Olives where Jesus' anguished prayer is punctuated by a moment of violence and then his arrest (22:39-54a). Peter's denial (22:54b-62), the mockery of Jesus by his captors (22:63-65), and a morning interrogation by the Sanhedrin (22:66-71) form the next cluster of scenes, each of them picking up motifs from the passover discourse and moving the story forward towards its resolution.

The trial before Pilate (23:1-25) is another important scene for Luke. After an initial interrogation by Pilate, Jesus is sent to Herod, a unique feature of Luke's account (23:6-12).

The scene ends with both rulers attesting Jesus' innocence, while the Jewish leaders and the assembled people choose Barabbas and condemn Jesus. The narrative mounts to its climax with the way of the cross during which Jesus addresses the women of Jerusalem (23:26-32)—another scene unique to Luke—and the crucifixion (23:33-49). Here Luke's theology of salvation is dramatically displayed in the repentance of the Good Criminal and in the heroic nature of Jesus' death. The burial by Joseph of Arimathea, a "good and just man," brings the Passion narrative to a quiet, and expectant, conclusion (23:50-56).

Our goal is not to explore the important historical questions that lie beneath the Passion account, but to draw out Luke's message from the manner in which he narrates the final hours of Jesus' life. In this narrative much of Luke's rich theology finds its most vivid illustration.

I. Betrayal: The Plot Against Jesus is Set in Place (22:1-6)

Turning abruptly from scenes of Jesus' teaching the crowds in the temple (19:47-21:38), Luke introduces the continuing determination of the leaders to kill Jesus and Judas' decision to provide the opportunity.

> [1]Now the feast of Unleavened Bread drew near, which is called the passover. [2]And the chief priests and the scribes were seeking how to put him to death; for they feared the people.
> [3]Then Satan entered into Judas called Iscariot, who was of the number of the twelve; [4]he went away and conferred with the chief priests and officers how he might betray him to them. [5]And they were glad, and engaged to give him money. [6]So he agreed, and sought an opportunity to betray him to them in the absence of the multitude.

The purpose of this opening scene is to draw the reader into the mood of the Passion story. Luke accomplishes this with short, quick strokes: the symbol-laden time of passover is evoked, Jesus' enemies are named, and the plot against his life set in motion. Even though Luke takes his cue from Mark's account, he still manages to put his own stamp on these introductory verses.

Timing is important in the Gospels and Luke begins his Passion story on that note. The feast of "Unleavened Bread, which is called the passover, was "approaching" (22:1). The feast of unleavened Bread continued for several days at the time of the barley harvest. Passover, originally a separate celebration, was a major pilgrimage feast that commemorated the liberation of Israel from slavery in Egypt. By the time of the New Testament, these two feasts were celebrated together, as Luke's text indicates.[1] Although explicit passover symbolism may not play a major role in Luke's description of Jesus' death, it looms large in the opening scenes of the Passion story. The next passage (22:7-13) describes preparation for the passover meal (the day "on which the passover lamb had to be sacrificed," 22:7). Luke will give special attention to the supper where Jesus speaks of the meaning of his impending death.

The Gospel's strong emphasis on salvation fits this passover symbolism. The Jesus who faces death is one whose advent inspired the strong salvation hymns of Mary ("God has put down the mighty from their thrones and exalted those of low degree. . . " 1:52) and Zechariah ("Blessed be the Lord God of Israel for God has visited and redeemed his people, and has raised up a horn of salvation for us. . . " 1:68-69). And Jesus himself had made a promise of liberation the keynote of his ministry ("He has sent me to proclaim

---

[1]See Fitzmyer, *The Gospel According to Luke X-XXIV*, 1369; I. Howard Marshall, *Commentary on Luke* 786-87. On passover and its relation to the last supper, see J. Jeremias, *The Eucharistic Words of Jesus* (New York: Scribner, 1966); I.H. Marshall, *Last Supper and Lord's Supper* (Grand Rapids: Eerdmans, 1981); A. Saldarini, *Jesus and Passover* (New York: Paulist, 1984); X. Léon-Dufour, *Sharing the Eucharistic Bread: The Witness of the New Testament* (New York: Paulist, 1987).

release to the captives ... to set at liberty those who are oppressed" 4:18). Later in the Gospel, at the Transfiguration, Jesus had conversed with Moses and Elijah about his "exodus which he was to fulfill in Jerusalem" (9:31). Using the term "exodus" to speak of Jesus' death (and resurrection) shows that Luke has linked the passover and the Passion. The liberating work of Jesus would find its "fulfillment" in his passage from death to life in Jerusalem. Now the moment of that liberation "approaches" (*ēggizen,* the expectant word that stands at the head of Luke's opening sentence) as the forces of death gather; that death will be a new passover, leading God's people from darkness to light.

This marking of the time knifes into the temple setting that had dominated Luke's narrative for three chapters. After a dramatic approach to the Holy City, Jesus had entered the temple, purifying it and making it the place of his final teaching (19:28-48). Luke frames the Temple setting with references to the forces that will strike at Jesus (see 19:47-48 and 22:1-2). But for the moment, Jesus commands his Father's House, "teaching the people ... and preaching the gospel" (20:1). One by one, groups of opponents are rebuffed and reduced to silence.[2] Jesus' teaching concludes with a discourse for his disciples (but "in the hearing of all the people," 20:45). Their fascination with the staggering beauty of Herod's masterpiece leads to Jesus' words of judgment on the temple (21:5-9) and the city of Jerusalem itself (21:20-24). The chaos and destruction they would experience would be only part of a more cosmic cataclysm ushering in the final consummation of history. Then the Son of Man would return triumphantly and the Kingdom of God would be finally established (21:25-36). In the midst of all this, the mission of the disciples would continue unafraid and unchecked, bolstered by the words which the Risen Christ would give them (21:10-19).

With the beginning of the Passion story, this vision of final victory over chaos and death abruptly swings back to

[2]Luke 20:1-8, 26, 40.

earth. The passover was approaching, and the struggle and victory the community had to expect would now first be experienced by their Lord.

Two sources of opposition to Jesus converge in this opening scene: the religious leaders and Satan who uses Judas as his agent. Luke identifies the leaders at this point as "the chief priests and the scribes" (22:2). These were two of the three groups that formed the ruling council or Sanhedrin. The third group, the "elders," will be mentioned later (22:66).

During the public ministry of Jesus Luke puts the Pharisees at the forefront of opposition to Jesus.[3] They are often joined by other groups (e.g., Scribes, lawyers) but they are a consistent element of those opposed to Jesus. Luke portrays them as lovers of money, greedy, and closed to the truth, personifying values counter to the Gospel, thereby giving us not a historical depiction of the Pharisees of Jesus' day but a stereotyped image of what a disciple is *not* to be. On the other hand, Luke is not as consistently negative about the Pharisees as the other Gospels. In 13:31-33 Pharisees warn Jesus about Herod's threat and in Acts Luke gives positive descriptions of Pharisees.[4]

When the action of the Gospel moves to Jerusalem, the "chief priests" emerge as the leading opposition group. The Pharisees make their last appearance as Jesus enters the Holy City; they demand that Jesus silence the acclaim his disciples give him (19:39). After entry into the city, however, the chief priests—again in company with other groups such as scribes or elders—take over (19:47). Historically, this is correct; the Sanhedrin, led by the priests, was the principal

[3]The Pharisees are in conflict with Jesus in the following scenes: 5:17-26, 29-32, 33-35; 6:1-5, 6-11; 7:36-50; 10:25-28; 11:37-41; 13:31-33; 14:1-6; 15:1-2; 17:20-21; 19:28-40. Jesus also directly criticizes the Pharisees in 11:42-44, 45-52; 12:1; 16:14-15; 18:9-14. On the role of the Pharisees, see J. Tyson, *The Death of Jesus in Luke-Acts*, 64-72.

[4]See, for example, Acts 5:33-39; 23:1-10. Paul is described as a Pharisee (Acts 26:2-29) and Pharisees are part of the Jerusalem church (Acts 15:5). Tyson's suggestion that the meals of Jesus with Pharisees help neutralize their negative image in the Gospel (J. Tyson, *The Death of Jesus in Luke-Acts*, 68) seems outweighed by the fact that at these meal settings Jesus severely criticizes his hosts and they are portrayed as in opposition to him (see, for example, 7:36-50; 14:1-24).

ruling body in Jerusalem and served as a mediating group between the Romans (who had direct political control of Judea and its capital, Jerusalem, in this period) and the Jewish population.[5] The shift from Pharisees in the public ministry to chief priests (and Sanhedrin) in the Jerusalem ministry was already part of Mark's narrative and Luke continues that format.

Jesus' opponents are seeking to destroy him but are at a loss on how to do it "because they feared the people" (22:2). Luke has sounded this theme before. Plots against Jesus begin early in the Gospel (see 6:11), smolder throughout many conflicts during Jesus' ministry in Galilee, and burst into flame when he reaches Jerusalem (19:47-48; 20:19). But those plots are fruitless because the "people" favor Jesus. While Luke's portrayal of the religious leaders is sharply negative, his portrayal of the "people" is more subtle. Luke uses two words to describe the general public: the "crowds" (the Greek word, *ochlos*, as in 23:4) or the "people" (*laos*, as in 22:2). The term "people" as used by Luke can have more significance, implying the corporate people Israel, not just a random assembly or a "crowd." Throughout most of the public ministry of Jesus and even into the final days in Jerusalem, the "crowds" and the "people" respond positively to him.[6] In fact, Luke contrasts the response of the people to that of the leaders, as in the case of Jesus teaching about John the Baptist: "When they heard this all the people (*laos*) and the tax collectors justified God, having been baptized with the baptism of John; but the Pharisees and the lawyers rejected the purpose of God for themselves, not having been baptized by him" (7:29-30). Right up to the very moment of the Passion this positive view continues. As Jesus is teaching in the temple, Luke observes, ". . . early in the morning all

---

[5]On the emergence of the Sanhedrin and its relationship to other institutions and movements in Judaism, see, S. Cohen, *From the Maccabees to the Mishnah* (Philadelphia: Westminster, 1987), esp. 104-23; also, R. Horsley & J. Hanson, *Bandits, Prophets, and Messiahs: Popular Movements at the Time of Jesus* (Minneapolis: Winston, 1986), esp. 1-47.

[6]E.g., Lk 4:42; 5:1,15; 6:19; 7:16; 8:40, 42; 11:14, 27-28; 12:40; 18:43, etc.

the people (*laos*) came to him in the temple to hear him" (21:38).

But this positive role of the crowds and people will take a cruel turn as the Passion continues. What began as a positive reaction to Jesus' mission sours in the Roman trial where the people join the leaders in rejecting Jesus (see, below, 23:18). Luke had signaled this turn of events in the opening scene at Nazareth: the first murmurs of admiration turn hostile as Jesus' provocative message sinks in (see 4:16-30). There is little doubt that Luke sees in this pattern the community's own destiny, when the mission to Israel met with little acceptance.[7]

But for now, at the beginning of the Passion, the people's allegiance to Jesus blocks the leaders' efforts to destroy him. That shield will be pierced by treachery, as Luke ushers on stage the figure of Judas (22:3-6). In Mark and Matthew, the story of the anointing stands between the plot of the leaders and Judas' betrayal, offering a pointed contrast between the woman's love for Jesus and the apostle's treachery.[8] Luke has already used the story of the anointing in a different context (7:36-50). As a result his Passion story opens with Judas' failure standing in the full glare of the spotlight.

The reason for this attention may be signaled in the opening phrase of verse 3: "Satan entered into Judas." Demonic power and not just the tragic failure of a disciple is at stake here. Satan who had left the Gospel stage at the conclusion of the temptation story (4:13) and had lurked behind the struggles of Jesus' public ministry, now reemerges as the driving power behind Judas.[9] Luke warns the reader again that the unfolding drama of death and victory involves more than the human arena; it is a cosmic drama effecting the destiny of the world. The evangelist will follow through

---

[7] Tyson refers to a pattern of "acceptance and rejection" experienced by Jesus on the part of the Jewish public in Luke. This same pattern will be continued in Acts; see, *The Death of Jesus in Luke-Acts*, 29-47.

[8] Compare Mark 14:1-11 and Mt 26:1-16; see the discussion in D. Senior, *The Passion of Jesus in the Gospel of Mark*, 43-49.

[9] See above, Part I, 31-35.

on this theme in the scenes that follow: Jesus will pray to rescue Simon and the other disciples from the "test" (22:31) and asks strength for himself as the "power of darkness" engulfs him (22:53).

But the role of Satan does not negate human responsibility. Once the demonic presence has been noted, Luke moves back to the sordid details of Judas' sin. He is introduced as "of the number of the Twelve." As we will discuss below (22:28-29), Luke gives special attention in his Gospel to the "Twelve Apostles." They are the special group that first walked with Jesus and will maintain continuity with the mission of Jesus as the Pentecost community takes up its mission in the world. Luke is painfully aware of Judas' place in this first community of Jesus.[10] When introducing their names he lists Judas Iscariot as the one "who became a traitor" (6:16). Replacing Judas in the circle of the Twelve becomes the first business of the post-Easter community (Acts 1:15-26). There Peter describes Judas as one who was "numbered among us, and was allotted his share in this ministry" (Acts 1:17), yet, inexplicably, became the "guide to those who arrested Jesus" (Acts 1:16).

Judas "leaves" to confer with the leaders. We are not told from where he leaves; presumably Luke means from the circle of Jesus' followers. Given the importance of 'following after" Jesus as the mode of discipleship in Luke (see, especially 9:23), the departure of Judas is equivalent to abandoning his discipleship.[11] This is exactly the way Peter describes him in Acts: "Judas turned asided to go to his own place" (Acts

---

[10]Some commentators suggest that by saying "of the number of the Twelve" Luke is trying to downplay Judas' membership, i.e., he was of the number but not really one of the Twelve (see Marshall, *Commentary on Luke*, 788). But Luke's emphasis on the tragedy of Judas and on his share in the ministry of the Twelve in Acts (see Acts 1:17, "For he was numbered among us, and was allotted his share in this ministry.") argues that Luke is highlighting, not down-playing, Judas' membership in the Twelve.

[11]See S. Brown, *Apostasy and Perseverance in the Theology of Luke* (Rome: Biblical Institute, 1969), 82-97. On discipleship in Luke, see R. O'Toole, *The Unity of Luke's Theology*, 191-265; C.H. Talbert, "Discipleship in the New Testament (Philadelphia: Fortress, 1985); 62-75; R. Tannehill, *The Narrative Unity of Luke-Acts*, 201-74.

1:25). Luke also hints at Judas' motivation. The chief priests and the "captains"[12] are delighted at this stroke of good luck and negotiate to give Judas' money. Although Luke is not as explicit as Matthew (Mt 26:15) and John (John 12:6) on Judas' greed, the frequent condemnation of greed and the corruptive love of money in this Gospel leaves little doubt that the evangelist draws a painful lesson here.[13]

The scene concludes with the consummation of Judas' apostasy. He agrees to the terms of betrayal and begins to "seek an *opportunity* to betray him to them in the absence of the multitude" (22:6). The figure of the traitor now merges with that of the demonic. Satan had left Jesus "until the *opportune* time." Judas' failure provides the opening for evil to work. In both instances, 4:13 and 22:6, Luke uses the root word *kairos*, "opportune time," a word suggesting not only the right moment, but in the New Testament, one frequently associated with the decisive time of the end of the world.[14]

Despite the pact among Satan, Judas and the leaders, the people's (Luke uses the term "crowd" in 22:6) love for Jesus is still a factor, so the opportunity must be in secret. Luke has set the stage for the events leading up to the arrest.

[12]Mark refers to "scribes." By "captains" Luke probably refers to leaders of the Temple security force under the control of the priests; see J. Fitzmyer, *The Gospel According to Luke X-XXIV*, p. 1375.

[13]Jesus warns his disciples, "Take heed, and beware of all covetousness; for a person's life does not consist in the abundance of their possessions" (12:15). The opponents of Jesus are described as "lovers of money" (16:14), while the disciples are told to go on mission with nothing, "no staff, nor bag, nor bread, nor money; and do not have two tunics" (9:3), and to trust in God rather than in human treasure (12:22-34). On the issue of possessions in Luke, see L. Timothy Johnson, *The Literary Function of Possessions in Luke-Acts* (Missoula: Scholars Press, 1977); R. Karris, "Poor and Rich: The Lukan *Sitz im Leben*," in C. Talbert (ed.), *Perspectives on Luke-Acts* (Macon: Mercer University, 1978), 112-25; R. O'Toole, *The Unity of Luke's Theology*, 129-35.

[14]In Luke see 1:20; 19:44; 21:8, 24. Reference to the final "time" may also be implied in 13:1; 18:30; 20:10 and 8:13 (a "time of test").

II. Passover: Jesus' Farewell to His Disciples (22:7-38).

The Passion story now moves to a series of passages that have great importance for Luke's theology. Luke has doubled the size of the passover meal account in comparison with the parallels of Mark and Matthew. The first scene, outside of Jerusalem, sets the stage: Jesus sends two apostles to prepare for the passover meal (22:7-13). The setting then shifts to the "large upper room" in Jerusalem where Jesus will celebrate a final passover with his apostles. At table Jesus celebrates the passover meal (22:14-20), and then begins a series of conversations or brief discourses with his followers: the prediction of Judas' betrayal (22:21-23), an instruction on authentic discipleship (22:24-30), a special prayer for Simon and the prediction of his denial (22:31-34), and a warning about the impending crisis of his death (22:35-38).[1]

Each of these segments are closely linked, and collectively they reveal Luke's special perspective on the meaning of Jesus' death.

> [7]Then came the day of Unleavened Bread, on which the passover lamb had to be sacrificed. [8]So Jesus sent Peter and John, saying, "Go and prepare the passover for us, that we may eat it." [9]They said to him, "Where will you have us prepare it?" [10]He said to them, "Behold, when you have entered the city, a man carrying a jar of water will meet you; follow him into the house which he enters, [11]and tell the householder, 'The Teacher says to you, Where is the guest room, where I am to eat the passover with my disciples?' [12]And he will show you a large upper room furnished; there make ready." [13]And they went, and

---

[1]A number of suggestions have been made about dividing this passage. Matera, for example, sees a threefold division based on the format of a farewell testament: a) 22:14-23, Jesus announces his death; b) 22:24-30, Jesus recalls his past life; c) 22:31-38, Jesus looks to the future (see F. Matera, *Passion Narratives*, 161-62). But such a topical arrangement seems a bit strained (Is, for example, 22:24-27 really about the "past life" of Jesus?). Some link verse 14 with the preparation scene rather than with the supper itself, as I do (see, also, Fitzmyer, *The Gospel According to Luke X-XXIV*, 1376). In any case it is a transitional verse between the two.

found it as he had told them; and they prepared the passover.

¹⁴And when the hour came, he sat at table, and the apostles with him.

¹⁵And he said to them, "I have earnestly desired to eat this passover with you before I suffer; ¹⁶For I tell you I shall not eat it until it is fulfilled in the kingdom of God." ¹⁷And he took a cup, and when he had given thanks he said, "Take this, and divide it among yourselves; ¹⁸for I tell you that from now on I shall not drink of the fruit of the vine until the kingdom of God comes." ¹⁹And he took bread, and when he had given thanks he broke it and gave it to them, saying, "This is my body which is given for you. Do this in remembrance of me." ²⁰And likewise the cup after supper, saying, "This cup which is poured out for you is the new covenant in my blood."

²¹"But behold the hand of him who betrays me is with me on the table. ²²For the Son of man goes as it has been determined; but woe to that man by whom he is betrayed!" ²³And they began to question one another, which of them it was that would do this.

²⁴A dispute also arose among them, which of them was to be regarded as the greatest. ²⁵And he said to them, "The kings of the Gentiles exercise lordship over them; and those in authority over them are called benefactors. ²⁶But not so with you; rather let the greatest among you become as the youngest, and the leader as one who serves. ²⁷For which is the greater, one who sits at table, or one who serves? Is it not the one who sits at table? But I am among you as one who serves."

²⁸"You are those who have continued with me in my trials; ²⁹and I assign to you, as my Father assigned to me, a kingdom, ³⁰that you may eat and drink at my table in my kingdom, and sit on thrones judging the twelve tribes of Israel."

³¹"Simon, Simon, behold, Satan demanded to have you, that he might sift you like wheat, ³²but I have prayed for you that your faith may not fail; and when you have turned again, strengthen your brethren." ³³And he said to

him, "Lord, I am ready to go with you to prison and to death." [34]He said, "I tell you, Peter, the cock will not crow this day, until you three times deny that you know me."

[35]And he said to them, "When I sent you out with no purse or bag or sandals, did you lack anything?" They said, "Nothing." [36]He said to them, "But now, let him who has a purse take it, and likewise a bag. And let him who has no sword sell his mantle and buy one. [37]For I tell you that this scripture must be fulfilled in me, 'And he was reckoned with transgressors'; for what is written about me has its fulfillment." [38]And they said, "Look, Lord, here are two swords." And he said to them, "It is enough."

A) PREPARATION FOR THE PASSOVER (22:7-14).

Luke draws the reader further into the Passion drama with this preparatory scene. There are only a few differences here between Luke's account and that of Mark, his major source.[2] The feast that was "approaching" in the opening verse of the Passion has now arrived (22:7). It is the "day of Unleavened Bread," the eve of passover and the afternoon on which the "passover lamb had to be sacrificed." As we noted above, Luke is very conscious of the fact that Jesus' Passion begins at the time of passover.[3] At the moment when Israel remembered its deliverance from the slavery of Egypt, God's new savior would begin his "exodus." The note of obligation—"*had to be* sacrificed"—is a point emphasized by Luke (compare Mark 14:12, "when they sacrificed the passover lamb"). The obligation flows from the Jewish law which required that each household "offer the passover sacrifice, in the evening at the going down of the sun, at the time you came out of Egypt" (see Deut 16:1-7). As faithful Jews, Jesus and his disciples will obey this law. But something else

[2]On Luke's essential connection to Mark in this scene, see J. Green, "Preparation for Passover (Luke 22:7-13): A Question of Redactional Technique," *Novum Testamentum* 29 (1987) 305-19.

[3]See the discussion under 22:1, above.

may be stirring beneath Luke's phrasing. The passover lamb "had to be sacrificed"—the Greek root word *dei* is used here, just as it was several times earlier in the Gospel in reference to Jesus' own sufferings.[4] In celebrating the passover and in going to his death, Jesus is in accord with God's redemptive will.

That sense of purpose is found in another distinctive aspect of Luke's scene. In Mark and Matthew it is the disciples who come to Jesus with the question of where the passover will be celebrated (see Mark 14:12; Mt 26:17); in Luke *Jesus* takes the initiative. Two of the Apostles, Peter and John, are sent on a mission: "Go and prepare the passover for us, that we may eat it." (22:8). These two, along with James, had been singled out before in the Gospel, to observe the raising of Jairus' daughter (8:51) and to be present at the trans-figuration (9:28). In the early chapters of Acts, Peter and John play the most prominent role in the mission of the Jerusalem community (Acts 3:1-11; 4:13-31; 8:14-25).

The whole thrust of the scene underscores Jesus' command of the situation. While his enemies plot against him and one of the Twelve squanders his discipleship, Jesus, deliberately and with calm control, prepares for the final passover. The majestic command and the obedient follow-through recall an earlier scene of the Gospel. When Jesus had reached Bethphage and Bethany on the Mount of Olives, he had sent two disciples to prepare for his entry into Jerusalem just over the crest (19:28-35). In that case, too, the precision of Jesus' instructions and their exact fulfillment gave him an aura of prophetic knowledge.

The two apostles selected for this mission carry it out faithfully (thereby serving the others, the model of disciple-ship that Jesus will endorse at the supper; see 22:7). A large upper room within the confines of Jerusalem (as the law dictated) is made ready. Luke marks the time: "And when the hour (*hōra*) came, he sat at table, and the apostles with him." (22:14). The decisive moment of the Passion is about

[4]See above, Part I, 35-39.

to strike. In the garden Jesus would tell his captors, "this is your hour (*hōra*), and the power of darkness" (22:53). But that "hour" belonged not only to the power of darkness; it was also the moment in which the death of the Son of Man would bring life to the world. Jesus' fragile community of "apostles," its ranks already shaken by betrayal, gathers with him.[5] And as a free man, Jesus "reclines" at table with them to celebrate the power of God's liberation.[6]

B) THE MEAL (22:15-20).

Jesus and his apostles are at table; the passover can begin. There is little doubt that this scene is of capital importance for Luke's Passion narrative. It is twice as long as the parallel accounts in Mark and Matthew. These evangelists frame Jesus' words of institution with the sharply contrasting predictions of betrayal, denial and desertion. Luke retains those components but rearranges them. The supper does not begin with the prediction of Judas' betrayal as in Mark and Matthew; instead attention is first given to Jesus' words about the meal itself (22:15-20). The prediction of betrayal comes after the meal (22:21-23), as the first of a series of statements Jesus makes to his apostles. Thus Luke has constructed a format of the meal (22:15-20), followed by a discourse (22:21-38).

[5] Mark and Matthew refer to the "Twelve"; Luke uses the term "apostle." In Mark and Matthew, Judas is clearly present for the supper and, in Matthew, even converses with Jesus (see Mt. 26:25). But Luke's account emphasizes the departure of Judas (22:3). Even though in 22:21 there is the implication that Judas may be present for the meal ("But behold the hand of him who betrays me is with me on the table"), the point is not stressed as in Mark and Matthew. Accordingly in 22:14 he does not refer to the "Twelve" but to "the apostles" as gathering for the supper; it is the faithful disciples, those for whom Jesus has prayed and whose faith will not fail (22:28-32), who gather for this final meal.

[6] Originally, the passover meal was to be eaten standing (see Exodus 12:11: "In this manner you shall eat it: your loins girded, your sandals on your feet, and your staff in your hand; and you shall eat it in haste."), but by the first century it was eaten "reclining" (the literal meaning of the Greek work *anepesen* which Luke uses here), the ordinary posture of the free person when eating at table and the right of every Israelite. See further, J. Fitzmyer, *The Gospel According to Luke X-XXIV*, 1384.

Because this is Jesus' last meal with his disciples before his death, his "discourse" takes on the poignant tones of a farewell speech. Recent studies have demonstrated that the format of a "farewell speech" was a well-known fixture of ancient literature which Luke adapted.[7] Although Greco-Roman classics used this device, too, Luke did not need to look much further than the Bible itself. Notable examples would be Jacob's deathbed speech to Joseph and his two sons in Genesis 48 and to the rest of his family in Genesis 49, or the final instructions of Moses to Joshua and the Israelites in the book of Deuteronomy (see, especially, chapters 31-34), or the last speeches of Joshua to the leaders (Joshua 23) and the tribes (Joshua 24).[8]

No single, fixed format is found in all of these examples but there are some standard features. Each involves an important leader who is conscious of impending death. Awareness of approaching death inspires the leader to instruct his or her disciples on the legacy left to them, on the shape of their own future, and on their responsibility to it.[9] A prime example of such a speech composed by Luke is Paul's address to the elders of the church of Ephesus (Acts 20:17-38). As Paul is about to disembark from the port of Miletus he gathers the elders and tells them of his impending imprisonment and probable death (Acts 20:20-25). He then reminds them of their responsibility to care for the church and warns them of the persecution they, too, can expect (20:28-30). The

---

[7]On this confer, J. Neyrey, *The Passion According to Luke*, 6-8; W. Kurz, "Luke 22:14-38 and Greco-Roman and Biblical Farewell Addresses," *Journal of Biblical Literature* 104 (1985) 251-68.

[8]These biblical precedents no doubt inspired the formats of non-biblical Jewish writing contemporary with Luke, such as *The Testament of the Twelve Patriarchs*, whose entire format is built on farewell discourses of the sons of Jacob, modeled on Genesis 49. For the text and commentary, see J. Charlesworth (ed.), *The Old Testament Pseudepigrapha*, Vol. 1 (New York: Doublday, 1983), 775-828.

[9]Neyrey suggests a basic four-part format for most New Testament examples of farewell discourses: 1) Prediction of death; 2) Predictions of attacks on leader's disciples; 3) Ideal behavior urged; 4) Commission. He cautions, however, against too rigid a conception of the form; see J. Neyrey, *The Passion According to Luke*, 7.

model for their ministry is Paul's own instruction and example (20:31-35).

There are two key components of the "farewell discourse" literary form at work in Luke's Passion narrative: (1) full consciousness of impending death or "departure" and (2) the leader's final instruction to his followers. Both of these components serve Luke's purposes in the Passion story. The last supper scene is, in effect, Jesus' final and most important prediction of his death and resurrection. And it is the occasion for a crucial instruction on the meaning of discipleship.

There is another aspect of Jesus' farewell discourse in Luke not found in many of the examples cited above—it takes place at a meal. This continues a pattern Luke establishes in the Gospel. Meals are some of the most frequent and most important settings for Jesus' teaching.[10] He is derided by his opponents as a "wine bibber and glutton" (7:34), because of his willingness to eat with sinners (5:29-32). Feeding the hungry crowds is not only a meal but a teaching parable on the meaning of the Kingdom of God (9:12-17). And, after the resurrection, meals would be a way of demonstrating Jesus' abiding presence with the community (24:28-32; 24:36-49).[11]

Here is the genius of Luke's account of the last supper: food and instruction blend together.[12] The ritual of the passover meal which Jesus and his apostles celebrate together, the new meaning given to the bread and wine by Jesus' words, and his after-dinner instructions to his disciples—all of these, word and food together, offer powerful, sustaining nourishment as the crisis of the Passion is about to break over the church.

The account of the supper itself has two distinct segments; the first (vs. 15-18) strongly reflects the passover ritual and is Jesus' final, prophetic prediction of his death and resurrection. The second (vs. 19-20) gives a new interpretation to the

[10]See, for example, 7:36-50; 10:38-50; 11:37-52; 14:1-24. On this see, R. Karris, *Luke: Artist and Theologian*, 47-78; J. Neyrey, *The Passion According to Luke*, 8-11.

[11]See below, pp. 156-57.

[12]See J. Neyrey, *The Passion According to Luke*, 10-11.

bread and wine based on the meaning of Jesus' death, and commands the community to reenact this meal in Jesus' memory. The two segments are linked by their parallel references to eating and drinking. We will discuss each segment in turn.

Verses 15-18:

The previous scene directed the reader's attention to the passover. Jesus had dispatched Peter and John to prepare for the feast in Jerusalem, and when the "hour" had arrived and all was ready, Jesus and the apostles took their places at table (22:7-14). The opening verse of this scene picks up this same focus, now framed in the words of Jesus himself: "I have earnestly desired to eat this passover with you before I suffer" (22:15). Jesus is fully conscious of what lies ahead. The fierce determination that had set his face toward Jerusalem (9:51) and brushed aside the threats of Herod (13:33) still burned within him. He would celebrate one final passover with his disciples, those who had walked with him from the beginning. That feast in which Israel remembered God's past deliverance from slavery in Egypt and looked forward to final salvation would be the perfect setting for Jesus' last instruction on what his own life and death meant. Note that it is not just the endpoint of death that hovers before Jesus; it is the entire Passion, "before I suffer" (*pathein*). This formulation is unique to Luke among the Gospel writers and is a hint that the entire Passion—all of Jesus' suffering—has, in Luke's prespective, redemptive force.

As throughout the Gospel, the Lukan Jesus foretells not only his death but his ultimate victory. The two verses that follow proclaim that message, first in terms of eating and then in connection with drinking:

"...I shall not *eat* it until it is fulfilled in the kingdom of God...(22:16)

"...I shall not *drink* of the fruit of the vine until the Kingdom of God comes" (22:17).

At this point in Luke's text there is no reference to the Eucharist; that comes only with verses 19-20. The eating and drinking mentioned in verses 16-17 are connected with the celebration of passover. The eating of the paschal lamb and its accompanying herbs, and the drinking of cups of wine interspersed throughout the ceremony form the heart of the passover rite.[13] Although Luke's account does not spell this out in detail, Jesus' opening statement leaves no doubt that the meal being described is the passover.

That passover setting gives the proper significance to Jesus' words. He celebrates with his disciples Israel's memory of past deliverance from slavery. That deliverance involved struggle: tearing loose from the tentacles of Pharaoh and his armies, traveling through the purifying stretches of the desert, groping for a sense of common purpose, and, finally, fighting for a stake in the land of promise. That exodus became the paradigm for every act of deliverance Israel had experienced in its long and tortuous history. Passover was not an act of nostalgia for things past but a point of reference for the future. What God had done for Israel in Egypt would be brought to completion on the final day of history. Passover, therefore, was thanksgiving for the past and an act of hope for the future.

That dual focus underlies Jesus' words at the supper. Now a new "exodus" was being enacted. Luke had used that term in the transfiguration story, as Moses and Elijah converse with Jesus about his death (see 9:31). In his own being Jesus would experience death and deliverance. In the context of the passover the language shifts to the symbolism of a meal. Because death would lash out at the messiah, there is a sense of "no more": "I shall *not* eat. . . ", "I shall *not* drink." Death would deprive Jesus of the nourishment and joy he enjoyed at table with his disciples. But because of God's fidelity, that life-giving fellowship would be restored. Jesus' exodus hopes would find fulfillment and, therefore, the "no more" of death is tempered by the "until" of hope: "*until* it is fulfilled in the kingdom of God," "*until* the kingdom of God comes."

When, in Luke's perspective, will the kingdom of God

---

[13]For details of the passover ritual, see the literature cited above, p. 42, n. 1.

come? When would Jesus' eating and drinking with his followers resume? In concert with all of New Testament theology, Luke sees the final consummation of the kingdom coming at the end of time, when the Son of Man would return in triumph (Luke 21:27; Acts 1:11). Peter describes this final moment of consummation in his sermon to the people in the portico of the Jerusalem temple: "Repent, therefore, and turn again, that your sins may be blotted out, that times of refreshing may come from the presence of the Lord, and that he send the Christ appointed for you, Jesus, whom heaven must receive until the time for establishing all that God spoke by the mouth of his holy prophets from of old" (Acts 3:19-21).

But Luke also sees the reality of the kingdom breaking into the world before that final day. The Risen Christ is present with the community and suffuses it with vital energy and purpose through the power of the Spirit. In this sense Jesus could say, "The kingdom of God is in the midst of you." (Luke 17:21). So in the experience of the community, the kingdom of God comes with the resurrection of Jesus. Then in a true sense the hopes embedded in the passover rite were already being "fulfilled" and the joyous bonds of life celebrated at that meal were renewed. That perspective is confirmed in the way that Luke stresses the Risen Jesus' table fellowship with the disciples. In the breaking of the bread, the two disciples who have left Jerusalem for Emmaus have their hopes restored (24:28-35), and by eating some of their broiled fish the Risen Jesus convinces the Jerusalem community of his renewed presence with them (24:38-43). The ecstatic meals of the Jerusalem community in Acts (2:47-48) continue this mood of post-Easter joy. Therefore, for Luke's theology, the resurrection of Jesus is the first stage in the realization of God's kingdom.[14]

---

[14]See below, "From Suffering to Glory," pp. 152-60; on eschatology in Luke, see R. Maddox, *The Purpose of Luke-Acts,* 100-57.

Verses 19-20:

Before considering the meaning of this passage we have to acknowledge that some ancient manuscripts omit these words altogether (beginning with "which is ... in verse 19 and extending through "in my blood" of verse 20), leading to the conclusion that these eucharistic words were not part of Luke's original Passion narrative. But more recent scholarship is moving strongly in the other direction. Far more important manuscript evidence supports the inclusion of these verses, and with their inclusion the perspective of Luke in the entire supper scene is clarified. That is the position we will take here.[15]

If these verses are to be included, however, we are still left with the question why Luke seems to repeat Jesus' actions over the bread and the wine. The difference is that in this segment Luke shifts the focus from the passover celebration to that of Eucharist. The passover symbolism of victory over death is not abandoned, however; the words of institution are fused onto the passover meal. Luke, in effect, draws a straight line from the community's celebration of Eucharist, back to the death and resurrection of Jesus, and further still to God's saving acts on behalf of Israel.[16]

[15]The primary evidence for this is the fifth or sixth century manuscript Codex Bezae. This manuscript has a number of variations in it, usually by way of addition or expansion. However, in the case of Luke 22:19b-20 it omits these words, an example of what is called a "western non-interpolation"—"western" because Codex Bezae was considered a prime example of a "western" manuscript tradition, "non-interpolation" because usually this tradition added material whereas in this case it omits it. Influential 19th century scholars took this as evidence that the shorter text of Luke 22 must therefore represent the older version. Most modern textual critics challenge this view, however; the text of Codex Bezae should not outweigh much more important manuscript evidence for the inclusion of 22:19-20. See K. Aland and B. Aland, *The Text of the New Testament* (Grand Rapids: Eerdmans, 1987), 306, and the discussion in J. Fitzmyer, *The Gospel According to Luke X-XXIV*, 1387-89.

[16]There is debate among scholars whether the last supper was historically a passover meal. Because John's chronology is different and because elements of the passover ritual are only lightly present in the gospel narratives (especially in the cases of Mark and Matthew), many scholars have suggested that this last meal was not a passover but some other kind of celebration. Whatever may be the case historically, there is no doubt that Luke (as with Mark and Matthew) presents this

Luke's formulation of Jesus' words over the bread and wine is different in some respects from that of Mark (and Matthew). The most significant are: 1) the addition of the words, "which is given for you," in reference to Jesus' body (vs. 19); 2) the words over the cup, especially the reference to "the new covenant in my blood." In general, Luke's version is closer to the tradition found in Paul (I Corinthians 11:23-26).[17] This is not to suggest that Luke is using Paul's letter as his model, but that a liturgical tradition similar to Paul's may have been the custom in Luke's community. Under that influence, the evangelist edited the last supper story he received from Mark.[18]

Many studies of this passage are interested primarily in its contribution to a theology of Eucharist or with the historical evolution of the Eucharist. As important as these issues are, neither of them will be the focus here. Since we are seeking an understanding of Luke's Passion story, our concern will be how these verses fit into Luke's narrative, and what light they throw on his understanding of the death of Jesus.

It is good to recall that Jesus' words to his apostles are in the context of a "farewell discourse" whose major purpose is

last supper as a passover meal and intended passover symbolism as an interpretive context for Jesus' words and actions.

[17]The distinct formulations of each tradition can be seen in the following line-up:
a) *Mk 14:22, 24:*
"Take; this is my body."
"*Drink of it, all of you; for* this is my blood of the covenant, which is poured out for many *for the forgiveness of sins.*
b) *Mt 26:26, 28:*
"Take, *eat*; this is my body."
c) *Luke 22:19, 20:*
"This is my body *which is given for you. Do this in remembrance of me.*"
"This *cup* which is poured out for you is *the new covenant in my blood.*"
d) *I Cor 11:24, 25:*
"This is my body which is for you. Do this in remembrance of me."
"This cup is the new covenant in my blood. Do this, *as often as you drink it*, in remembrance of me."

[18]See a similar conclusion in J. Fitzmyer, *The Gospel According to Luke X-XXIV*. 1386-95. This does not mean that Luke was using an entirely different source other than Mark or that all the changes in the text can be assigned to the liturgical practice of Luke's church. Many of the changes reflect Luke's theological perspective which he wants to proclaim in the Passion story.

to leave his followers with a true sense of his legacy to them.[19] Jesus' words over the bread and the cup are another prediction of his impending death, but even more important, they reveal to his disciples the inner meaning of his death.

The Bread

Luke first describes an action and follows with an explanatory word. With ritual gestures, Jesus takes a loaf of bread, gives thanks (Luke uses the words *eucharistēsas* here), breaks the bread and gives it to his disciples. The words give meaning to his action: "This is my body which is given for you." Jesus, who by countless acts of mercy had nourished people throughout the Gospel and who had fed hungry multitudes (the wording of 22:19 is meant to recall that incident, see 9:16), now feeds them again. The food is Jesus himself—not Jesus as an abstraction, but Jesus in the act of "giving" himself for his disciples. This is an element of Luke not found in Mark or Matthew: the words "given for you" make explicit what the actions of breaking and distributing signify. Jesus' death is to be understood not as an arbitrary act of violence, not as a senseless waste, but as a death on behalf of others. Jesus dies for those he loves. Luke's use of the word "for you (plural)" both here and in the words over the cup (where Mark and Matthew use the words "for many") intensifies the personal bonding of Jesus with his disciples. He dies for them.

The Cup

For a second time at the meal, there are words of thanksgiving over the cup and it is distributed to the apostles (see 22:17). This action is curtly summarized with Luke's "likewise the cup after supper" in verse 20. But the explanatory words are drawn out. The cup is identified as a cup "poured out for you." Once again the image of death on behalf of those Jesus loves is evoked.

---

[19]See, above, p. 54.

But something more is added here. The pouring out of the cup is not only an image of Jesus' death but of what that death effects: it is "the new covenant in my blood." Mark's tradition ("This is my blood of the covenant," 14:24) had already connected the pouring out of Jesus' blood with the "covenant." In Exodus 24 the great sealing of the covenant between Yahweh and Israel takes place with a blood ritual. Moses sprinkles the blood of sacrificed oxen on the altar and then on the people: "Behold the blood of the covenant which the Lord has made with you in accordance with all these words" (Ex 24:8). On that covenant rested Israel's hopes for salvation. God's life (symbolized in the blood on the altar) and Israel's destiny (symbolized in the blood sprinkled on the people) were fused together. Early in the Gospel Luke recalls the covenant with Abraham, another foundation of Israel's hope: ". . . to remember [God's] holy covenant, the oath which God swore to our father Abraham, to grant us that we, being delivered from the hand of our enemies, might serve God without fear, in holiness and righteousness before God all the days of our life." (1:72-75). Peter recalls that same covenant image in his temple sermon:

> "You are the children of the prophets and of the covenant which God gave to your ancestors, saying to Abraham, 'And in your posterity shall all the families of the earth be blessed.' God, having raised up his servant, sent him to you first, to bless you in turning every one of you from your wickedness." (Acts 3:25-26).

Luke's reference to the "*new* covenant" seems to draw as well from Jeremiah:

> "Behold, the days are coming, says the Lord, when I will make a new covenant with the house of Israel and the house of Judah, not like the covenant which I made with their ancestors when I took them by the hand to bring them out of the land of Egypt, my covenant which they broke, though I was their husband, says the Lord. But this is the covenant which I will make with the house of Israel

after those days, says the Lord: I will put my law within them, and I will write it upon their hearts; and I will be their God, and they shall by my people. And no longer shall each person teach their neighbor and each their brother or sister, saying, 'Know the Lord,' for they shall all know me, from the least of them to the greatest, says the Lord; for I will forgive their iniquity, and I will remember their sin no more." (Jeremiah 31:31-34)

This rich passage has strong resonance with Luke's portrayal of Jesus' mission. Jesus' message of repentance and forgiveness embodies the renewal foreseen by Jeremiah. His death on behalf of the people is the indelible sign of God's covenant with Israel and ushers in the final and definitive period of salvation history.

Remembering

Between the words over the bread and the words over the cup, Jesus declares: "Do this in remembrance of me" (22:19). This emphasis on remembrance is special to Luke.[20] The phrase should be applied to both parts of the eucharistic action, the bread and the cup. The "likewise" of verse 20 helps extend Jesus' command to both actions.

These words turn the spotlight on the disciples. They are to "do this in remembrance of [Jesus]." The command takes the reader beyond the death of Jesus to the post-Easter community. As we shall comment later, the crucial function of the apostles is to provide that link between the time of Jesus and the post-Easter time of the church.[21] The very fact that Luke wrote Acts as a sequel to the Gospel demonstrates that the connection between the mission of Jesus and the mission of the church was a primary concern for him. Dynamic memory (*anamnesis*, in the Greek) was to be a primary means by which that connection would be maintained. "Remem-

[20]This is another similarity to the Pauline tradition; see I Cor 11:24-25, but it is absent in Mark and Matthew.

[21]See below, pp. 71-79.

bering" in this sense was not a matter of occasionally dusting off scenes from the past. Active reflection on Jesus' words and actions was sustained by the continuing presence of the Risen Christ in the community and by the power of the Spirit. That "remembering" was to color the community's perspective and help it to approach each situation in the spirit of Jesus.

Luke illustrates this kind of "remembering" in the Emmaus story, when Jesus rekindles the two disciples' hopes by reviewing his life in the light of the Scriptures (24:27). Significantly, the action of blessing, breaking and distributing the bread finally brings that memory of Jesus into focus (24:30-31).[22] Some of the apostles' sermons in Acts have a similar pattern. The appeal for repentance is accompanied by remembrance of God's acts of salvation in the past, climaxing with Jesus' own mission to Israel.[23]

In the context of the Passion story, the command to "Do this in remembrance of me" means more than continuing Jesus' practice of life-giving meals with disciples and outcasts. The "this" referred to should not be reduced simply to the liturgical action. Jesus had stated that the bread broken and the cup poured out is *himself* in the act of dying for others. It is this central act of Jesus' mission—the act that reveals the meaning of all his other actions—which the community is to "do in remembrance of me." In short, the Passion of Jesus becomes the model for the community's own life. In the rest of the farewell discourse and throughout the rest of the Passion narrative, Luke will reaffirm this basic conviction: The manner and spirit of Jesus' death are the touchstones for all authentic discipleship.

The last supper is, therefore, one of Luke's most important scenes. It reaches back to summarize the entire ministry of Jesus as a life given for others. It reaches forward in portraying the authentic spirit of the church as living in remembrance of the crucified and Risen Christ.

[22]See below, pp. 155-57.

[23]E.g., Acts 2:14-29; 3:12-26; 10:34-43; 13:16-41.

C) THE HAND OF THE BETRAYER (22:21-23).

Jesus' prediction of Judas' betrayal swings the reader's attention back fully upon the disciples. Judas' willingness to leave Jesus and to trade money for the life of his Master is a startling contrast with the emphasis on table fellowship in the previous verses. Luke is conscious of that jolting contrast in the way he words Jesus' prediction: "...the hand of him who betrays me is *with me on the table*" (compare Mark 14:20, "one who is dipping bread in the same dish with me").

Luke had already informed the reader that Judas' treachery was incited by Satan (22:3). But even this staggering brew of human treachery and demonic inspiration is not allowed to overpower Jesus. The Son of Man's death will, ultimately, not be explained as a triumph of evil. "For the Son of Man goes *as it has been determined*" (22:22). Mark and Matthew make similar affirmations but do it in terms of scriptural fulfillment ("as it is *written* of him," see Mark 14:21). For Luke even the experience of betrayal is part of God's mysterious plan of redemption to which Jesus is faithful without retreat.[24]

The demonic factor does not erase Judas' responsibility. Jesus pronounces a prophetic "woe" or warning of judgment upon the apostle who has violated his call. Throughout Luke's Gospel Jesus manages to couple words of forgiveness and mercy with words of prophetic judgment that bore into the conscience of his audience. "Woes" introduce condemnations for those whose lives contradict the values of the kingdom.[25] It is clear that Luke wants to make such an example of Judas. The troubled self-questioning that begins among the apostles ("which of them it was that would do this...") is intended to stir within the reader as well.

While Luke gives attention to the tragic specter of Judas,

[24]Here the Greek word *hōrismenon* ("determined") is used, as in Acts 2:23 where Peter speaks of Jesus as one "delivered up according to the definite (*hōrismenei*) plan and foreknowledge of God..." (see also Acts 4:28; 10:42; 17:26, 31). This term is similar in meaning to the verb *dei* frequently applied to the necessity of Jesus' death in Luke; cf. above, Part I, pp. 35-39.

[25]See Lk 6:24, 25, 26; 11:42, 43, 44, 46, 47, 52; 17:1.

one senses that his heart is not here. Unlike the accounts of Mark and Matthew, the prediction of Judas' betrayal is submerged in the overall flow of the supper account. By speaking of the betrayer's hand being "on the table" Luke implies that Judas is present. But Luke does not dwell on this. Nor will he include the description of Judas' death in the Passion story, as Matthew does.[26] It will be mentioned parenthetically in Acts to explain why the number of the Twelve needed to be restored. So, too, Luke's most urgent concern in the Passion story is not with Judas but with the Apostles who remain faithful. The rest of the discourse concentrates on them.

D) TRUE GREATNESS (22:24-30)

With penetrating irony, Luke has the very apostles who were shocked at the possibility of betrayal begin to argue among themselves about which of them was the greatest! As we will see, Luke does not want to paint a completely bleak picture of Jesus' disciples in the Passion story. But even so, their response to Jesus is hardly portrayed in ideal terms.[27]

The material in these verses has no direct parallel in the Passion accounts of Matthew or Mark. There are, however, important connections with material on discipleship that appears elsewhere in the other Synoptic Gospels. A similar dispute about greatness is found in Mark 10:35-45 and 9:33-37 (see Luke 9:46-48). The saying about the apostles being appointed judges of the twelve tribes is similar to Matthew 19:28. What Luke has done is to recast this material and place it here in the dramatic and highly symbolic setting of the last supper.

The apostles' absorption with their own importance runs directly counter to the message of love unto death proclaimed in the breaking of the bread and the pouring of the cup.

---

[26]On Mt 27:3-10, see D. Senior, *The Passion of Jesus in the Gospel of Matthew*, 104-108.

[27]See the detailed and balanced presentation in R. Tannehill, *The Narrative Unity of Luke-Acts*, 253-74.

Luke's insertion of the dispute immediately after the prediction of Judas' betrayal whiplashes the reader from the sublime to the tragic to the ridiculous. Jesus' response to the argument leads to another important segment of the farewell discourse.[28]

Exercise of leadership in the Christian community is sharply contrasted with leadership on the part of worldly powers. The kings of the Gentiles "lord it over" their subjects. The Greek verb used here, *kurieuousin*, derives from the root *kurios* or "lord." The implication is one of oppressive force: the power comes from the top down, on to the backs of the king's subjects.[29] The point is repeated in other terms: "those who exercise power over them are called benefactors." The verb here is *exousiazō*, from the root *exousia*, meaning power or authority. In this context, the sense again is that of overbearing power. This earns for the rulers the title of "benefactor," an honorific title used extensively in the first century Mediterranean world for potentates and powerful citizens.[30] One wonders if there is not an ironic note in Jesus' use of the term "benefactor" here.[31]

The Christian leader is not to be caught in this web of brutal power and self-aggrandizement. As was often the case in the Gospel, Jesus' words turn the values of the world

[28]Instruction on the virtues needed by disciples is a typical element in many farewell speeches; see J. Neyrey, *The Passion According to Luke*, 7.

[29]This is the only occurrence of the verb in the Gospels, but it is used by Paul with a similar connotation when speaking of the grip that sin and death exercise over human beings (as in Romans 6:9, 14). Paul also tells the Corinthians that he would not want to "lord it over" their faith (I Cor 1:24). But the verb is used in a more positive sense of authority, as in Romans 14:9 where Christ is described as ruling over the living and dead or I Tim 6:15 where Christ is acclaimed as "king of kings and lord of those who rule" (*kurieuonton*).

[30]Caesar, for example, was called a "benefactor." On this important aspect of Greco-Roman culture see, F. Danker, *Benefactor: Epigraphic Study of a Graeco-Roman and New Testament Semantic Field* (St. Louis: Clayton Publishing House, 1982). A more popular treatment of the influence of this notion on Luke's theology can be found in F. Danker, *Luke* (Proclamation Commentaries; Philadelphia: Fortress, 2nd rev. ed., 1987), 28-46.

[31]But see D. Lull, "The Servant-Benefactor as a Model of Greatness (Luke 22:24-30)," *Novum Testamentum* 28 (1986) 289-305, who contends that "benefactor" is presented as a positive example of greatness by Luke.

upside down. The "greatest" should become the "youngest."
The "leader" should become the "one who serves." The salvation proclaimed by Jesus disrupts people's expectations (in
this case, that of his own apostles). Mary's hymn had exalted
God who "scattered the proud in the imagination of their
hearts," and "...put down the mighty from their thrones
and exalted those of low degree" (1:51-52). And Simeon had
prophesied that Jesus would effect "the fall and rising of
many in Israel" (2:34). This is the note of "reversal" closely
associated with the prophetic tradition. The coming of God's
reign would be "good news to the poor" (see the quote from
Isaiah 61 in Luke 4:18), shattering the oppressive power
holding people in bondage.[32]

Now that searing prophetic critique is turned not on Jesus'
opponents but on his own apostles. The term "leader"
(*hēgoumenos*) suggests that Luke is thinking of offices within
the Christian community. In Mark's version of these sayings,
Jesus words are addressed more towards *aspirations* for
power. The desire of James and John to have places of glory
triggers the discussion. Jesus' response is directed to those
who "*would be* great" or who "*would be* first" (see Mark
10:43-44). But in Luke's version Jesus's words are directed to
those who are already in positions of responsibility within
the community ("let the greatest...", "let the ... leader"). In
Acts 15:22, the Jerusalem apostles and elders choose Judas
and Silas, "leaders (*hēgoumenous*) among the brethren," as
messengers to the church of Antioch. The mentality of the
Christian leader is not to be drugged with power; the most
important person ("the greatest") is to be as the "youngest,"
that is, as the person with the least status within the community. The "leader," the person with the most authority, is
to be as "one who serves," that is, as one who takes orders
from others and seems to have no authority.

The meal imagery so important to Luke and dominant in

---

[32]On this "eschatological revolution" see, E. Schillebeeckx, *Jesus: An Experiment
in Christology* (New York: Seabury, 1979), 172-78; F. Danker, *Luke*, 47-57.

this part of the Passion narrative now takes over.[33] Mark's version of this scene climaxed with a key saying of Jesus: "For the Son of Man also came not to be served but to serve, and to give his life as a ransom for many." (Mk 10:45).[34] The exercise of power within the Christian community must be modeled on the life-giving service of Jesus, a service most vividly demonstrated in his death for others. Luke accepts this same premise. But "serving" (*diakonein*) is not left generic as in Mark's version. The model Luke has in mind is that of serving at table: "For which is the greater, one who sits at table, or one who serves? Is it not the one who sits at table? But I am among you as one who serves." (22:27). Obviously the one who sits to enjoy the meal seems to be in a better position than the one who has to serve it. But again there is a reversal of perspective. Jesus' place within the community of the disciples is not as honored diner but as "one who serves."

On other occasions in Luke's Gospel, Jesus had drawn from table manners lessons about siding with the powerless. In the parable of the feast (14:7-11), those jostling for the best seats have to give way to others, while those in the lowest places are publicly honored by the host and invited to move up. The moral is clear: "For those who exalt themselves will be humbled and the ones who humble themselves will be exalted" (14:11; see a similar saying in 18:14). The following instruction on drawing up a guest list for a banquet moves in a similar vein (14:12-14). Invite to your banquet not the rich or influential who are liable to be a good investment for your hospitality but the "poor, the maimed, the lame, the blind." Kindness to these powerless people will be rewarded "at the resurrection of the just" (14:14).

---

[33] There is a similarity between this scene and that of the footwashing in John 13:1-20. In John's account Jesus' washing the feet of the disciples is not only an example of service (see John 13:12-17), but symbolizes the redemptive power of his death (John 13:6-11, "If I do not wash you, you have no part in me.") Both levels—discipleship instruction and image of redemptive death—are also present in Luke's version, as we shall see.

[34] On the importance of this saying for Mark's christology, see D. Senior, *The Passion of Jesus in the Gospel of Mark*, 33.

Jesus lived what he taught. The words over the bread and wine at the passover meal had revealed the deepest motivation of his mission. Not only did he serve the disciples, his very life was the food: "This is my body...", "This cup ... is the new covenant in my blood" (22:19-20). Those words captured the meaning of his death and the inner spirit of his entire life. He was not the potentate lording it over others and exploiting them, but the servant who gave his life for others. Luke's Gospel is aware that this way of exercising power runs counter to the normal experience of the world. It is captured in Jesus' simile about the marriage feast (12:35-40). Here servant imagery is applied to the coming of the Son of Man at the end of time. "Blessed are those servants whom the master finds awake when he comes; truly, I say to you, he will gird himself and have them sit at table, and he will come and serve them." The "lord" (*kurios*) becomes the "servant" (*doulos*) who serves (*diakonesei*) them at table. The same vocabulary and the same startling reversal of roles is found here as in the saying at the last supper.

Some interpreters consider it significant that Luke does not seem to use all of the original Markan saying which inspired this scene. In Mark's version Jesus speaks of himself not only as the one who comes to serve but as one "who gives his life in ransom for the many" (Mk 10:45). Is Luke downplaying the redemptive meaning of Jesus' death by omitting this reference? While the evangelist does not use the explicit image of atonement (i.e., giving one's life in ransom), it would be a mistake to conclude that Luke does not ascribe redemptive significance to Jesus' death.[35] The immediate purpose of the saying in 22:27 is to present Jesus as the servant model for the exercise of authority in the community. The redemptive power of Jesus' death has already been proclaimed loud and clear in this scene in the words over the bread and the cup. Given that context, it is also clear that the image of "servant" applies to Jesus' death. Offering his life

---

[35]See the various positions described in J. Kodell, "Luke's Theology of the Death of Jesus," in D. Durken (ed.), *Sin, Salvation, and The Spirit*, 221-30.

for others is Jesus' ultimate act of table service, that is, it has redemptive significance.

E) THE REWARDS OF PERSEVERANCE (22:28-30).

The discourse continues its focus on the apostles and once again the mood shifts. Despite their hunger for acclaim, the apostles are blessed because they have remained faithful to Jesus. In the scene that follows (22:31-34), the reader is reminded that perseverance, too, is a gift.

The vocabulary and images used here are typical of Luke. The apostles are characterized as those "who have continued with me in my trials" (22:28). The notion of continuing on a journey with Jesus dominates Luke's Gospel.[36] Discipleship means following Jesus from the beginning, witnessing his mission, absorbing his teaching, and remaining with him through difficulty and trial, even through death itself. In so doing the disciple becomes a "witness," and is able to proclaim the gospel of Jesus to the world. This is precisely what Peter tells the assembled college of apostles as they prepare to choose a replacement for Judas: "So one of those who have accompanied us during all the time that the Lord Jesus went in and out among us, beginning from the baptism of John until the day when he was taken up from us—one of these must become with us a witness to the resurrection" (Acts 1:21-22). By contrast, Judas is one "who turned aside, to go to his own place" (Acts 1:25).

In the context of the Passion, the call to follow Jesus focuses on the experience of "trials" (22:28). As we have already noted, the ministry of Jesus was filled with conflict.[37] Luke's Gospel is aware that the opposition which struck at Jesus would also buffet his followers. "Blessed are you when people hate you, and when they exclude you and revile you, and cast out your name as evil, on account of the Son of Man! Rejoice in that day, and leap for joy, for behold, your

[36]See above, Part I, pp. 36-39.
[37]See above, Part I, pp. 28-31.

reward is great in heaven; for so their fathers did to the prophets" (6:22-23). To share in Jesus' mission was also to share in his rejection: "He who hears you hears me, and he who rejects you rejects me. . . " (10:16). Luke follows through in Acts. The Jerusalem apostles meet opposition, persecution, even death itself (e.g., Acts 4:1-4; 5:17, 26-42; 6:12-8:1; 8:3). Paul, the "chosen vessel," has opposition and threat as his traveling companions (e.g., 9:23). In his farewell speech to the elders of Ephesus, Paul, too, will speak of the "tears . . . and trials" (Acts 20:19 *peirasmōn,* the same word used by Luke in 22:28) that marked his mission, just as it had the mission of his Master.

The Passion would be the final "trial" of Jesus, but conflict and suffering were already familiar to him. The struggle with death would be the definitive struggle with evil, but that conflict had already spilled over into Jesus' apostolic sufferings.[38] In Luke's portrayal of the Passion, the apostles, even though weak and uncomprehending, continue to follow Jesus and would never leave him. Fidelity to him through death would be their lifeline and would define their crucial function in the founding of the post-Easter community. One of the amazing features of Luke's narrative is the manner in which he clings to this basic portrait of the apostles, even though the Passion tradition received from Mark moves in a decidedly different direction. In Mark's Passion story, the disciples fail, abandoning Jesus and their discipleship.[39] Matthew moderates his overall portrayal of the disciples but does not attempt to reverse the basic picture of their abandonment of Jesus at the time of the Passion.[40] As we will see, to assert the ultimate perseverance of the apostles in the Passion, Luke will have to omit references to their flight at the time of the arrest and hint at their distant presence as the Passion reaches its climactic scene. Jesus' words at the supper lay the foundation for Luke's entire portrayal of the apostles.

[38]See above, Part I, pp. 31-35.
[39]See D. Senior, *The Passion of Jesus in the Gospel of Mark,* pp. 148-55.
[40]See D. Senior, *The Passion of Jesus in the Gospel of Matthew,* pp. 172-75.

Two regal consequences flow from the apostles' fidelity to Jesus: They will eat and drink at Jesus' table in the kingdom and they will be enthroned as judges over the twelve tribes of Israel (22:30).

From the first lines of the Gospel, Luke depicts Jesus as the royal messiah who fulfills the promise of unending strength and protection given to Israel through the Davidic monarchy. The angel Gabriel declares that Mary's child will be called by a royal title, "Son of the Most High" and "the Lord God will give to him the throne of his father David, and he will reign over the house of Jacob forever; and of his kingdom there will be no end" (1:32-33). The announcement of God's reign is the leitmotif of Jesus' entire ministry (see, for example, 4:43).[41]

Luke draws on this royal imagery at the last supper. As members of Jesus' royal retinue, the apostles will share in the glory of his kingdom. But once again meal imagery becomes dominant. The apostles will "eat and drink at my table in my kingdom" (22:30). It is interesting to conjure up a picture of that glorious kingdom banquet on Luke's own terms. The image is not that of Jesus and his apostles dining alone in royal splendor. Earlier in the Gospel others were already given invitations to this same banquet. At the house of a Pharisee, one of Jesus' table companions had exclaimed: "Blessed is the one who shall eat bread in the kingdom of God!" (14:15). Jesus responds with the parable of the great banquet in which the invited guests decline to come, and their place is taken by "the poor and maimed and blind and lame" gathered from the street, and when places still remain, by those collected from "the highways and hedges" (14:21-23). A similar vision of guests coming from beyond the boundaries prompted Jesus' words, "And the people will come from east and west, and from north and south, and sit at table in the kingdom of God" (13:29). The kingdom banquet is crammed with the "uninvitable;" and such is the banquet where places will be held for the battered yet still

---

[41]See, J. Fitzmyer, *The Gospel According to Luke I-IX*, pp. 149-50.

faithful apostles. In Luke's Gospel, dining in the kingdom is a metaphor of inclusion, not of privilege.[42]

The apostles are also enthroned as judges over the twelve tribes of Israel. A similar saying is found in Matthew's Gospel, "Truly, I say to you, in the new world, when the Son of man shall sit on his glorious throne, you will also sit on twelve thrones, judging the twelve tribes of Israel" (19:28). The strong future thrust of Matthew's version ("in the new world") is also found in Luke. The apostles who persevere with Jesus through the trials of conflict and death will go with him to the end of that journey, communion with God in the fullness of the kingdom.[43] The symbol of the "twelve tribes" also has a future cast to it. The full assembly of the tribes had shredded in tragedy long before in Israel's history. Their regathering in the land of Israel was one way of expressing hope for final salvation.[44] The faithful apostles are promised a leadership role in that future community.

Although Luke's material shares in the future, eschatological flavor of the saying in Matthew, there is also a decidedly present thrust to it. Jesus' words concerning the apostles' dining in the kingdom and their appointment as judges are firm and immediate: "I appoint for you..." (22:29).[45] While the image of the kingdom banquet evokes the final destiny of Jesus and the apostles, it also colors Luke's image of the church in the present age. Thus after the resurrection, the apostles begin to dine with Jesus. The

[42]See J. Neyrey, *The Passion According to Luke*, pp. 8-9 and R. Karris, *Luke: Artist and Theologian*, pp. 58-65.

[43]The role of the ascension is important in Luke (see Luke 24:50-53; Acts 1:9-11), signifying the ultimate destiny of Jesus as he returns in triumph to God.

[44]K. Rengstorf, "*dōdeka*" in G. Kittel (ed.), *Theological Dictionary of the New Testament*, Vol. 2 (Grand Rapids: Eerdmans, 1964), pp. 321-28; C.K. Barrett, *The Signs of An Apostle* (Philadelphia: Fortress, 1972); R. Brown, *The Critical Meaning of the Bible* (New York: Paulist, 1981), 126-29.

[45]Some interpreters see an echo of covenant terminology in Luke's verb for "appoint" (*diatithemai*), thus continuing the notion of "new covenant" introduced at the supper (see 22:20). In some ancient manuscripts the word "covenant" (*diathē ken*) is actually used: "I appoint for you a covenant...." On this, see J. Fitzmyer, *The Gospel According to Luke X-XXIV*, 1419.

Emmaus disciples have their hearts glow when the Risen Christ breaks bread with them (24:28-35), and the rest of the apostles are ecstatic to share broiled fish with him (24:36-43). That special table fellowship with the apostles is mentioned by Peter in Acts, "...but God raised him on the third day and made him manifest; not to all the people but to us who were chosen by God as witnesses, who ate and drank with him after he rose from the dead." (Acts 10:40-41). The un-shattered love bond between the Risen Christ and his faithful followers will reach full expression in the heavenly banquet, but, now in the present age, it nourishes and sustains the leaders of the new community.[46]

Under the terms of this new covenant the apostles are appointed as "judges" over the tribes of Israel. The judges of Israel were not understood in biblical tradition solely in a legal sense. They were charismatic leaders, rallying the tribes for their defense and administering justice. As the community's turbulent history begins to unfold in Acts, this is precisely the role the apostles will play. Filled with the power of the Spirit they stir up the crowds and bring them to repentance (Acts 2:37). They guide the community and help it perceive the work of the Spirit in unexpected events (Acts 11:1-18). And on more than one occasion, the apostles are called upon to make judgments for the good of the community (e.g., Acts 6:1-6, the selection of deacons). This work of the apostles confirms Jesus' promise to them at the last supper. And it also shows that Luke sees the swelling post-easter community as the establishment of the new Israel. Once again in Luke's perspective, events awaited at the end time begin now to explode into history.

F) SIMON'S CRISIS (22:31-34).

The role of Peter in all four Passion narratives is fascinating. If Judas provides a chilling illustration of apostasy and absolute failure, Peter is an example of how loyalty,

---

[46]On the resurrection appearance stories in Luke, see below, pp. 152-60.

weakness, and ultimate redemption can all co-exist in one human history.

Satan, who had entered into Judas and driven him to betray Jesus (22:3), also seeks out Peter and the rest of the apostles (the two pronouns "you" in vs. 31 are plural in the Greek). Luke portrays evil as aggressive and rapacious. The demon "demands" the disciples; the Greek word *exēitēsato* implies a bold and arrogant attack by Satan.[47] The "trials" which Jesus endures (22:28) will also engulf his followers. Satan wants to "sift [them] like wheat" (v. 31). This striking metaphor implies that the power of evil wants to utterly control them, tossing them helplessly in the air like cut wheat. Some interpreters see another level of meaning here; the sifting of wheat is an act of sorting the grain from the chaff. Therefore Luke might mean that Satan wants to separate the apostles from Jesus. This would be equivalent to Jesus' prediction of denial and desertion in Mark and Matthew, where Jesus speaks of them being "scandalized" in him and being "scattered" (see Mk 14:26-31; Mt 26:30-35).[48] In any case, it is clear that Luke sees the power of Satan as diametrically opposed to that of Jesus.[49] Satan holds people bound (e.g., 13:16) and Jesus has come to rescue them. During the crisis of suffering and death Satan's final assault will be mounted against those whom Jesus has chosen to be his witnesses.

In verse 32 the focus shifts from the entire band of apostles to Peter alone (the "you" in verse 32 is singular). Jesus had addressed the leader of the apostles by his pre-conversion

[47]The word is used with this connotation in the *Testament of Benjamin* 3:3, "Even if the spirits of Beliar seek to derange you with all sorts of wicked oppression, they will not dominate you, any more than they dominated Joseph, my brother." (See further, I.H. Marshall, *Commentary on Luke*, 820). Others have noted a similarity to the opening scene of Job (1:6-12), but in Job God is the one who gives permission to Satan for a testing of Job. In Luke's Passion story, the power of evil is presented in much more aggressive terms.

[48]See, J. Fitzmyer, *The Gospel According to Luke XI-XXIV*, 1424. There may be an allusion to Amos 9:9, "For lo, I will command, and shake the house of Israel among all the nations as one shakes with a sieve, but no pebble shall fall upon the earth." However, a different Greek verb is used in the Septuagint (Greek) version of this text so that the connection to Luke is less likely.

[49]See above, Part I, pp 31-35.

name, "Simon," perhaps an indication that Peter's identity as a follower of Jesus is at stake.[50] The crisis for Peter (and, by implication, for all of the disciples) will be a near failure of faith. Peter will be tempted to deny that he even knows Jesus (22:34), equivalently a violation of the very foundation of his discipleship.

Jesus' prayer for Peter (v. 32) is a distinctive feature of Luke's scene. Satan's assault on the disciples is checked by the power of Jesus' prayer. The scars of that struggle will be visible, as Peter's hollow words of bravado (22:33) and the account of his denial will make clear (22:54-62). Peter will fail miserably and must "turn again." Luke's unusual formulation implies that Peter's faith in Jesus will bend dangerously, but will not break. The verb used for repentance here (*epistrepsas*, to "turn") has echoes in other parts of Luke's two volume work. The brother or sister who sins seven times in the day and yet "*turns* to you seven times saying 'I repent'" is to be forgiven (17:4). In Acts this equation between "turning" and "repentance" is repeated.[51] Therefore even the serious failure of denying one's discipleship out of fear need not be a terminal sin, if one is open to repentance.

The decisive element is Jesus' prayer; without it Peter would succumb to the power of evil. The power of that prayer will not only draw Peter back from the brink of doom but recommission him as the leader of the apostolic community. After Peter has repented he must "strengthen" the brethren (22:32).[52] Their need for Peter's support implies that the rest of the apostles will not be exempt from Satan's attacks. "Strengthening" the community is an act of pastoral leadership that Paul will perform in his mission journeys through

---

[50]In the listing of the twelve, Luke refers to "Simon, whom he [Jesus] named Peter" (6:14).

[51]As in Peter's sermon in Acts 3:19, "Repent, therefore, and turn again"; see also, 9:35; 11:21; 14:15; 15:19; 26:18, 20.

[52]This important role given to Peter is Luke's equivalent for the Petrine blessing found in Matthew 16:16 (which is omitted in Luke); see further, R. Brown, K. Donfried, J. Reumann, *Peter in the New Testament* (Mahwah: Paulist, 1973), pp. 120-25.

Asia Minor (see the same verb in Acts 18:23). Although the identical wording is not used, Peter is certainly presented in Acts as a pillar of strength for the Jerusalem community, as he preaches boldly and endures persecution because of the Gospel.

Peter's destiny of failure and renewal are yet to be played out, so here Jesus' words wash over him without his comprehension. Despite Jesus' warning, the apostle confidently asserts his unyielding fidelity: "Lord, I am ready to go with you to prison and to death" (22:33). The wording reflects Luke's perspective. In the parallel passages of Mark and Matthew, Peter speaks of not "being scandalized" in Jesus (see Mk 14:29; Mt 26:33). Luke casts this into his favored "journey" imagery: "I am ready to go with you to prison and death."[53] Peter's repeated imprisonment for the sake of the Gospel will be narrated in Acts (see Acts 4:1-3; 5:17-21; 12:3-11); there is no mention of his death. But before the apostle will be so tenaciously committed to Jesus, he will experience failure and repentance. That is the sharp thrust of Jesus' prophetic words: "I tell you, Peter, the cock will not crow this day, until you three times deny that you know me" (22:34).

The subtle threads in Luke's portrayal of the apostles are close to the surface here. Because he views the apostles as the vital link between the mission of Jesus and the life of the post-Easter community, Luke does not present them as completely broken by the events of the Passion. Hence there is no mention of the scattering of Jesus' followers in the prediction scene (contrast Mk 14:27; Mt 26:31; Jn 16:32). Nor will there be any reference to their flight at the moment of arrest. In the account of Peter's denial, Luke alone will mention that Jesus looks directly at the apostle and provokes his repentant tears (22:61-62). And Luke hints that his followers were present at the cross (23:49).

But the supper scene guarantees that Luke does not intend to idealize the apostles either. The responsibilities of leader-

---

[53]See above, Part I, pp. 37-39.

ship are severe.[54] But those called by Jesus prove to be a very fallible group. One of their number betrays Jesus, their leader denies him, all of them will argue about their own greatness, and all of them are vulnerable to the power of evil. From the first moments of Luke's Gospel, this realistic, mixed portrait is in evidence. After the marvelous catch of fish—a catch Peter had been skeptical about—the apostle recoils from Jesus, "Depart from me, for I am a sinful man, O Lord" (5:8). The unfolding story of the Gospel and Acts proves that this is not polite formality for Luke. Peter *is* a sinful man, but he is also chosen to follow Jesus. Through Jesus' prayer, this fallible apostle will "turn" and become the one who rallies the Jerusalem church at Pentecost, directs the explosive mission of the young church, and guides the community through its most important pastoral decision concerning the inclusion of Gentiles.[55]

G) PREPARING FOR THE FINAL STRUGGLE (22:35-38).

The passover meal and Jesus' farewell discourse now come to a conclusion. The next scenes of Jesus' prayer and the terrible moment of arrest will plunge the reader into the depths of the Passion. This final passage of the discourse heightens the tension of impending conflict and shapes it into an urgent warning to the apostles.

Jesus recalls the mission instructions he gave earlier in the Gospel (see the sending of the twelve in 9:1-6 and the seventy in 10:1-12). In these first days of the mission they needed no provisions for their mission travels: "no staff, nor bag, nor

---

[54]The demands on "those who have been given much" are put in stringent terms in Luke: see, for example, Lk 12:41-48; 16:10-12.

[55]"...a test of fidelity can come even to one who will prove to be the 'greatest' among them [the apostles], the one most ready to protest of his readiness to go with Jesus to prison or to death. The Lucan Jesus is making it clear to the reader of the Gospel that no disciple, not even the one for whom Jesus has prayed, will be safe from a test to his/her loyalty and fidelity." J. Fitzmyer, *The Gospel According to Luke XI-XXIV*, p. 1423.

bread, nor money; and do not have two tunics" (9:3); "no purse, no bag, no sandals" (10:4). The power of the word and the support of the homes they would evangelize were enough. They lacked "nothing" (22:35).

"But now. . ." (22:36) the mission was entering into its critical phase; the struggle between the power of life and the power of death was about to break into the open. For this cosmic struggle the apostles would need resources. If someone has a purse, they should bring it with them, and a bag also. If someone has no sword, they should even sell their mantle to get one. Everyone must be equipped for the struggle.[56]

The impending conflict between Jesus and his opponents was no accident; it, too, was part of God's mysterious plan of salvation. Luke drives that lesson home by means of a fulfillment quotation (22:37). Jesus cites Isaiah 53:12 where the suffering servant is depicted as having "poured out his soul to death, and was numbered with the transgressors; yet he bore the sin of many, and made intercession for the transgressors." Luke centers on one element of this quotation: the "reckoning" of Jesus with transgressors (literally, "lawless ones," *anomoi*). The precise meaning of this reference is not immediately clear. Who are the "transgressors" referred to? The two thieves crucified with Jesus (23:32-33)? Or Barabbas? Or does Luke intend to refer to the sword-bearing apostles in the next scene? Or, more widely, the sinners Jesus allied himself with in the Gospel?

Some clarity may come with the fact that it is not Jesus or his apostles doing the "reckoning" but his opponents (as is the case with the Servant in the original quote from Isaiah). Identifying Jesus with the transgressors is another expression of hostility toward him and proof that his enemies do not believe in him, reminiscent of 7:33 where his opponents said, "Behold, a glutton and a drunkard, a friend of tax collectors and sinners!" Jesus' association with the "lawless" had galled the religious leaders throughout the entire Gospel. The same

---

[56]On the translation of this difficult verse, see the detailed discussion in J. Neyrey, *The Passion According to Luke*, 37-39.

hostility toward Jesus and misinterpretation of his mission would infest those who come to arrest him ("Have you come out as against a robber, with swords and clubs?" 22:52) and prompt their calumnious accusations at the trial ("We found this man perverting our nation, and forbidding us to give tribute to Caesar, and saying that he himself is Christ a king." 23:2).

To be "reckoned with the transgressors," therefore, should not be reduced to one or other scene or set of characters in the Gospel. This hostile view of Jesus is what enables his enemies to justify their efforts to destroy him. But the reader who has traveled the long journey of this Gospel from Galilee to Jerusalem, and who will continue that story through into the history of the community in Acts, knows that there is an element of irony in this judgment against Jesus. He *was* reckoned with the transgressors—not simply in the twisted view of those who would kill Jesus, but also in the sense that Jesus chose to be with the "lawless." In his consorting with the tax collectors and sinners Jesus was fulfilling the Scriptures in a profound sense, bringing God's salvation to "all flesh," especially those "sick" and helpless ones in need of mercy. That mission would be enacted one more time in the Passion story, as Jesus, crucified between two criminals, will bring with him into paradise one who repents.[57]

Buy a *sword*—that threatening command is a key element of this passage and one that needs careful interpretation. Within the story itself, the apostles understand Jesus literally: "Look, Lord, here are two swords." (22:38). But is the literal meaning the correct one? The wider context of the Passion story and of the Gospel itself suggests that "sword" is used in a metaphorical sense here. In the next scene, at the moment of arrest, Jesus explicitly rejects the use of the sword. He heals the violence inflicted by one of his disciples and commands: "No more of this!" (see, below, 22:49-51). This rejection of violence accords with Jesus' teaching earlier in the Gospel on love of enemies and refusing retaliation for injury.[58]

---

[57]See below, 23:39-43.

[58]See Luke 6:27-36. On the love of enemies tradition, see W. Klassen, *Love of*

On the other hand, Luke has already used "sword" as a metaphor for conflict. Simeon tells Mary that "a sword will pierce through your own soul" (2:35), a prophecy of the suffering to be endured because of her association with Jesus (a "child set for the fall and rising of many in Israel, and for a sign that is spoken against," 2:34). Further evidence for the equivalence of "sword" and "conflict" for Luke may be found in his version of another saying of Jesus. In Matthew 10:34, Jesus says, "Do not think I have come to bring peace on earth; I have not come to bring peace, but a sword." The subsequent verses interpret what "sword" means: divisions within the family because of commitment to the Gospel (see Mt 10:35-36). In his parallel to this verse, Luke's version reads: "Do you think that I have come to give peace on earth? No, I tell you, but rather *division*." (Lk 12:51). "Division" is Luke's interpretation of the "sword" symbol in Matthew's version.[59]

Therefore, at the conclusion of the supper, Jesus warns his disciples to be prepared for conflict. They will need new resources on the journey that looms before them, because the power of evil and resistance to the message of the Gospel will assault them. The sufferings of Jesus' Passion and the persecution the community will endure in its mission confirm this prediction of Jesus.

Whereas Jesus speaks metaphorically of needing a "sword" for this cosmic struggle, the apostles prove uncomprehending. They think that two real swords will be enough. Just as Peter had miscalculated the power of evil in the previous passage (22:29), now the rest of the apostles underestimate the kind of threat facing them. Jesus' words are curt with frustration: "Enough!" His response is not to be confused

Enemies: The Way to Peace (Overtures to Biblical Theology, Philadelphia: Fortress, 1984); J. Piper, *'Love Your Enemies' Jesus' Love Command in the Synoptic Gospels and the Early Christian Paraenesis* (Cambridge: Cambridge University, 1979).

[59]On the meaning of these and other conflict sayings in Luke, see D. Senior, "The New Testament and Peacemaking: Some Problem Passages," in *Faith and Mission* 4 (1986), 71-77; G. Lampe, "The Two Swords (Luke 22:35-38)," in E. Bammel and C.F.D. Moule (eds.), *Jesus and The Politics of His Day* (Cambridge: Cambridge University Press, 1984), 335-52.

with approval of the apostle's weaponry. The wording in the Greek echoes the angry words of Yahweh to Moses in Deuteronomy 3:26: "But the Lord was angry with me on your account, and would not harken to me; and the Lord said to me, 'Let it suffice you; speak no more to me of this matter.'"[60]

The final passover has been celebrated. Now the Passion begins. Despite Jesus' instruction at the meal, the apostles do not realize what their Master faces nor do they comprehend how their own destiny will be entwined with his. Understanding comes only in the light of resurrection. Then the presence of the Risen Christ and the power of his Spirit would make his words glow within their hearts (24:32).

III. The Mount of Olives: Jesus' Struggle in Prayer (22:39-46) and His Arrest (22:47-53).

Jesus had concluded his discourse at the supper with a warning to his disciples to be prepared for a massive struggle (22:35-38). Now, as the scene shifts to the Mount of Olives, that decisive test engulfs Jesus and his followers. Jesus' prayer in agony (22:39-46) and his nighttime arrest (22:47-53) signal that the full force of the Passion has begun.

> [39]And he came out, and went, as was his custom, to the Mount of Olives; and the disciples followed him. [40]And when he came to the place he said to them, "Pray that you may not enter into temptation." [41]And he withdrew from them about a stone's throw, and knelt down and prayed, [42]"Father, if thou art willing, remove this cup from me; nevertheless not my will, but thine, be done." [43]And there appeared to him an angel from heaven, strengthening him. [44]And being in an agony he prayed more earnestly; and his sweat became like great drops of blood falling down upon the ground. [45]And when he rose from prayer, he came to the disciples and found them sleeping for sorrow, [46]and he said to them, "Why do you sleep? Rise and pray

[60]The same root work *ikanos* is used in both texts.

that you may not enter into temptation."

[47]While he was still speaking, there came a crowd, and the man called Judas, one of the twelve, was leading them. He drew near to Jesus to kiss him; [48]but Jesus said to him, "Judas, would you betray the Son of man with a kiss?" [49]And when those who were about him saw what would follow, they said, "Lord, shall we strike with the sword?" [50]And one of them struck the slave of the high priest and cut off his right ear. [51]But Jesus said, "No more of this!" And he touched his ear and healed him. [52]Then Jesus said to the chief priests and officers of the temple and elders, who had come out against him, "Have you come out as against a robber, with swords and clubs? [53]When I was with you day after day in the temple, you did not lay hands on me. But this is your hour, and the power of darkness."

A) JESUS' STRUGGLE IN PRAYER (22:39-46)

While Luke draws much of his inspiration for this scene from Mark, there are sharp differences between the two accounts.[1] Luke's version is much briefer than Mark's. It does not mention Gethsemani but only a generic location on the "Mount of Olives" (22:39). The special role of Peter, James and John is omitted (compare Mk 14:33), nor does Jesus shuttle back and forth to rouse the sleeping disciples. Even more important, Luke offers only a single prayer instead of the repeated prayers found in Mark and Matthew. References to Jesus' sadness are omitted. On the other hand Luke adds a reference to Jesus' "agony" and reports the appearance of a comforting angel. These changes give Luke's version a very distinctive character, one that fits well into the

---

[1]On the Gethsemane tradition in general, see R. Barbour, "Gethsemane in the Tradition of the Passion," *New Testament Studies* 16 (1969/70) 231-51; J.W. Holleron, *The Synoptic Gethsemane: A Critical Study* (Analecta Gregoriana: Rome: Gregorian University, 1973); D. Stanley, *Jesus in Gethsemane* (New York: Paulist, 1980); A. Feuillet, "Le récit lucanien de l'agonie de Gethsemani (Lc xxii. 39-46)," *New Testament Studies* 22 (1976) 397-417.

major motifs of his Passion story.

Jesus comes to the Mount of Olives, the place where he had lodged each night during his time in Jerusalem (21:37). Luke's wording underlines the presence of the same disciples who had been the recipients of his instruction at the passover meal: "and the disciples followed him" (22:39).[2] The instruction about the threat of crisis will continue, now with the eloquence of Jesus' own example.

The overall shape of the scene makes it an instruction on the need for prayer in crisis. When they reach the mount of Olives, Jesus tells his followers: "Pray that you may not enter into temptation" (22:40). Those words are followed by Jesus' own departure ("about a stone's throw") for intense prayer (22:41-44). Upon his return, he finds the disciples' sleeping; he rouses them by repeating the opening instruction: "Rise and pray that you may not enter into temptation" (22:46). Thus the scene has a clear structure: Jesus' words on the necessity of prayer to survive the "test" surround his own example of urgent prayer.

A key word for the entire scene is that of "temptation" or, more accurately translated, "test." The underlying Greek word *peirasmos* denotes a sense of struggle and trial rather than seduction. Luke used this term to characterize the assaults of Satan against Jesus at the beginning of his ministry (4:2, 13). The devil's attempts to divert Jesus from his messianic mission is a deadly test of strength on whose outcome the salvation of the world depended. After failing to defeat Jesus, the demon had suspended those direct assaults, biding time until the opportune moment of the Passion (4:13).[3]

The fierce and tenacious threat of evil was such that only God's power could overcome it. Unprepared, the disciple would be overwhelmed by such "tests," as Jesus warns in the

---

[2]Compare Mark who simply notes, "They (Jesus and the disciples) went to a place called Gethsemane...", (Mk 14:32), and Matthew, "Jesus went with them..." (Mt 26:36).

[3]Through conflicts and exorcisms during the public ministry of Jesus, however, the demonic presence is still felt. The Passion represents a renewed and definitive attack of evil in Luke's perspective; see above, Part I, pp. 31-35.

parable of the sower, where the seeds that fell on rocky soil
are interpreted as those "who, when they hear the word,
receive it with joy; but these have no root, they believe for a
while and in time of test (*peirasmou*) fall away" (8:13). In the
model of prayer Jesus gives to the disciples he, therefore,
instructs them to ask the Father: "lead us not into the test
(*peirasmon*)" (11:4).

As we have already noted, Luke conceives of the Passion
itself as the final "test" of Jesus.[4] Here the faithful Son of
God enters into the final struggle with the power of evil. At
the passover meal the disciples were warned of this impending
combat and told to "arm" themselves for it (22:35-38). The
faithful disciples would be those who persevered with Jesus
in his "trials" (*peirasmois*, 22:28). Now in the guise of death,
the power of evil would tear at Jesus and his fragile community like some unrelenting storm. Only the might of God
could withstand such vicious power. Thus the command to
pray is no mere formality; it is the absolute means for sur-
vival.

Luke portrays Jesus as the embodiment of his own instruction. Where Mark and Matthew present Jesus racked with
grief and distress before the onslaught of death, Luke's scene
has a different tone. In the ancient world, the emotion of
grief could have a connotation of weakness.[5] It was one of
the four classic "passions" considered a disorder in popular
Hellenistic philosophy. "Grief," in the cultural context of the
ancient world, meant shrinking from impending struggle or
combat. The threat of death made one collapse in fear. Some
traditions of Jewish thought considered grief as a sign of
punishment for sin or as a symptom of guilt.

Luke screens all mention of grief from his account of
Jesus' final prayer.[6] Nor does Jesus collapse on the ground

---

[4]See above, 22:28, and Part I, pp. 32-33; also the discussion in S. Brown, *Apostasy and Perseverance*, 5-34.

[5]On this see J. Neyrey, *The Passion According to Luke*, 50-53; J.M. Ford, *My Enemy is my Guest*, 116-120.

[6]See Mark 14:33-34, ". . . (he) began to be greatly distressed and troubled. And he said to them, 'My soul is very sorrowful, even to death' . . ."; similarly Mt 26:37-38.

as he does in Mark's account (Mk 14:35; in Mt 26:39, he falls on his face). Luke states that Jesus "knelt down and prayed" (22:41). And he does not reach out for the comfort of his disciples, as is the case in Mark and Matthew.

Jesus faces death courageously, without fear. Although the request to "remove this cup from me" still remains—a prayer for deliverance from the test as in the Lord's prayer (11:4)—it is clearly subordinated to the basic theme of the prayer: "Father ... not my will, but thine, be done."[7] Jesus, God's champion and obedient Servant, kneels with self-control and dignity, to pray for the strength and courage to follow God's will even into the jaws of death.[8]

Luke continues this portrayal in the next verses, where an angel from heaven comes to "strengthen" Jesus, while Jesus himself prays "in agony," his sweat becoming "like great drops of blood falling down upon the ground" (22:43-44). These verses are missing in some later manuscripts and some scholars consider them an addition to Luke's original version. Although it is impossible to be definitive about this, there seems no good reason to eliminate these verses—either on the ground of manuscript evidence or their harmony with Luke's perspective.[9] In fact the appearance of the comforting angel and the references to "agony" and "sweat" fit well into Luke's emphasis on Jesus' test.

The angel's appearance is, in effect, God's answer to Jesus' courageous prayer. Throughout his Gospel, Luke refers to

[7]Note that Luke also inserts the phrase "if thou art willing" alongside the prayer for deliverance from the cup (compare Mk 14:35, "if it were possible" and 14:36, "all things are possible"; Mt 26:39, "if it be possible"). Luke's version clearly emphasizes the primacy of the divine will.

[8]Possible influence on this scene by the Suffering Servant motif found in Isaiah is noted by J. Green, "Jesus on the Mount of Olives (Luke 22:39-46): Tradition and Theology," *Journal for the Study of the New Testament* 26 (1986) 29-48 and W.J. Larkin, "The Old Testament Background of Luke xxii, 43-44," *New Testament Studies* 25 (1979) 250-54.

[9]See the discussion in J. Fitzmyer, *The Gospel According to Luke IX-XXIV*, 1443-44; also J. Neyrey, *The Passion According to Luke*, 55-57, both of whom support the authenticity of this verse. Arguments against authenticity are summed up in B. Ehrman and M. Plunkett, "The Angel and The Agony: The Textual Problem of Luke 22:43-44," *Catholic Biblical Quarterly* 45 (1983) 401-16.

angels.[10] Messenger angels are major characters in the infancy gospel, announcing God's plan of salvation to Zachary, Mary, and the shepherds. In other instances, "angels" are used as an indirect way of referring to God's own presence (see 12:8, 9; 15:10). In the Passion, the "angel from heaven" comes to "strengthen" Jesus. The most intense moment of the prayer is at hand. Jesus is "in agony" and "sweats" profusely. Both details fit into a description of Jesus' prayer as a moment of fierce struggle with the power of death.[11] "Agony" was understood in the ancient world not as fear or excruciating pain or distress, as the word might seem to us at first glance. The Greek term *agōnia* was used to describe "victorious struggle" of the athlete or warrior.[12] The reference to "sweat" contributes to this sense of ultimate exertion. Luke does not say that Jesus actually perspired in blood; rather he uses a vivid simile: his exertion was so great that his sweat became "*like (hōsei)* great drops of blood falling down upon the ground" (22:44). The evangelist has a knack for such colorful metaphors throughout his Gospel.[13]

His moment of intense prayer and struggle completed, Jesus stands up and returns to his disciples (22:45). They sleep "for sorrow" (22:45). In Mark's version, Jesus had interrupted his prayer three times to return to the disciples, each time discovering them asleep (see Mk 14:37, 40, 41). Mark's account portrays the disciples as weak, failing to be awake and "watching" for the approach of the decisive hour of the Passion.[14] In Luke's version the spotlight does not fall quite as harshly on the chronic dullness of the disciples; they do

[10]See, for example, multiple references in the infancy narrative, plus 4:10; 9:26; 12:8, 9; 15:10; 16:22; 20:36; 24:33.

[11]Thus Jesus is not without emotion in Luke's account, but it is emotion connected with tense struggle rather than grief or fear. Neyrey's characterization of Jesus in this scene may be too stoic. See the comments of J. Green, "Jesus on the Mount of Olives," 29-48.

[12]See J. Neyrey, *The Passion According to Luke*, 58-59.

[13]Satan, for example, wanted to "sift [Peter] like wheat" (Lk 22:31). For list of other such comparisons in Luke see J. Neyrey, *The Passion According to Luke*, 64.

[14]See D. Senior, *The Passion of Jesus in the Gospel of Mark*, 77-80.

not directly contravene Jesus' command to "stay awake" (see Mark 14:34, 37). Yet Luke does portray them as weak. Jesus struggles in prayer like God's champion, thrusting aside the assaults of evil that would sway him from his mission. But the disciples crumple in "grief," sleep overtaking them when they should have been fortifying themselves in prayer for the test ahead.

The conclusion of the scene reaffirms its basic message: "Rise and pray that you may not enter into the test" (22:46). In the course of his ministry Jesus had taught the necessity of praying "always and without losing heart" (18:1). His message was urgent in his final teaching in the temple:

> "But take heed to yourselves lest your hearts be weighted down with dissipation and drunkenness and cares of this life, and that day come upon you suddenly like a snare; for it will come upon all who dwell upon the face of the whole earth. But watch at all times, *praying that you may have strength to escape all these things that will take place,* and to stand before the Son of man." (21:34-36).

In the Passion Jesus was faithful to his own teaching. Fired with God's strength through prayer, Jesus the martyr-prophet and obedient servant of God is ready to face death. It would not catch him unaware. The disciples, their faith still weak and untested, would ultimately survive the trauma of suffering and death only because of Jesus' prayer on their behalf (22:32). After the wrenching disillusion of the Passion would come the triumph of the resurrection. Then the bold strength of the Spirit, the final gift of the Risen Christ, would be poured into their hearts.

B) THE ARREST (22:47-53).

The warnings have been sounded; Jesus' intense prayer for strength has been completed. Now the wave of opposition will break upon Jesus and his disciples. Luke's rendition of the arrest scene is briefer than Mark's and taut in its narration. The focus narrows to the sharp contrast between the spirit of Jesus and that of the armed band that comes to seize him.

Luke emphasizes the connection to Jesus' prayer by the way he introduces the scene ("While he was still speaking...", 22:47). Jesus' warning about the need to pray is confirmed by the intrusion of the power of death into the scene. Judas, the disciple whose apostasy Jesus had already predicted (22:21-22), "leads" the crowd who come to arrest Jesus. Luke's subtle emphasis on the leadership role of Judas inflames the terrible wound that the memory of Judas must have been for the early community.[15] Luke's narration is lean; we are not told in advance what Judas' plan was (compare Mark 14:44). It is Jesus who reveals his disciple's treachery. As Judas attempts to kiss his master, violating the sacred sign of friendship, Jesus brings him up short: "Judas, would you betray the Son of Man with a kiss?" (22:48). Jesus is in control, even in such a violent moment as this.

Unlike Mark and Matthew, Luke does not allow Judas' kiss to be the moment for the arrest. In fact, the poisonous kiss is never consummated. Much more important for Luke is the outbreak of violence that follows; here the true contrast between Jesus and his opponents is clearly in view. In Mark's version the use of a sword seems to be an act of chaotic violence, originating not from a disciple but by one of the armed mob that comes to arrest Jesus ("one of those who stood by," see Mark 14:47).[16] Matthew identifies the attacker as a disciple ("one of those who were with Jesus," Mt 26:51) but still depicts it as an impulsive response to the arrest of Jesus (see 26:50, "...they came up and laid hands on Jesus and seized him").[17]

In Luke's account, however, the decision to use a sword in Jesus' defense is deliberate. Those who are on Jesus' side ask

[15]Compare Mark (14:43) and Matthew (26:47) who note that Judas came "and with him a . . . crowd."

[16]For a discussion of this text, see D. Senior, *The Passion of Jesus in the Gospel of Mark*, 82-83.

[17]See D. Senior, *The Passion of Jesus in the Gospel of Matthew*, 85.

the key question: "Lord, shall we strike with the sword?" (22:49). Without waiting for an answer, a disciple slashes at the high priest's slave, severing his right ear (22:50).[18] Jesus' response is characteristic of Luke's Gospel. He immediately halts the use of violence on his behalf: "No more of this!"[19] And then, without a word, he heals the slave's ear (22:51). The gesture is eloquent. Jesus the healer, heals even his enemies who come to arrest him and mark him for death.[20]

There is no doubt that Luke intends this scene to be an instruction on the use of violence and retribution. The deliberate question of the disciple reflects the early community's own concern with the question of violence: "Lord, shall we strike with the sword?"[21] The response to that question had already been given earlier in the Gospel:

> "But I say to you that hear, Love your enemies, do good to those hate you, bless those who curse you, pray for those who abuse you. To the one who strikes you on the cheek, offer the other also; and from the one who takes away your coat do not withhold even your shirt.... But love your enemies, and do good..." (6:27-29, 35).

Now as Jesus himself suffers violence he refuses to retaliate or to have violence used on his behalf. Instead, he returns compassion and love for enmity. Once again, he is faithful to his own teaching. But the disciples had already displayed their ignorance of Jesus' teaching at the passover meal. When Jesus had used the image of a sword as a metaphor for

---

[18]Both Luke and John include the detail that it was the slave's "right" ear; see John 18:10. Luke adds a similar detail in the story of the man with the withered arm; he notes it was his "right hand" (compare Mk 3:1, "a withered hand").

[19]The Greek phrase used here—*eate heos toutou*—is difficult to translate. Literally it means, "let it be, up to this point." The sense is that of an order to stop the violence: "enough," "no more."

[20]On the important role of healing in Luke's Gospel, see above Part I, pp. 33-34.

[21]On the issue of non-violence in Luke's Gospel and the New Testament in general, see the literature cited above, p. 81, n. 58. This issue in Luke is a major concern of J. Ford, in her study, *My Enemy is My Guest*; for this text, see pp. 120-21.

readiness in face of the impending test, they had taken him literally (see 22:38). While Jesus struggled courageously in prayer, they had slept out of grief and fear (22:45).

The scene concludes with Jesus' words to his captors. Luke identifies this "crowd" (22:47) as "the chief priests and captains of the temple and elders" (22:52). In Mark's version the armed mob is sent "from" the Jewish leaders; in Luke the leaders themselves come to seize Jesus. Luke's version is improbable from a historical point of view, but his depiction of the scene allows him to still consider the general crowds of people as neutral or even favorable to Jesus. Only at the trial will they be swayed to decide against Jesus.[22] The Jerusalem authorities, on the other hand, have already shown their hostility against Jesus. When he taught in the temple, they had sought "to destroy him." But the people "hung upon his words" and they were afraid to move against Jesus (19:47-48). But now their hostility against Jesus had boiled over and, emboldened by Judas' treachery and under the cover of darkness, they come "with swords and clubs" to arrest Jesus. They treat Jesus as if he were a "robber," thus partially fulfilling Jesus' own prediction at the passover meal: "For I tell you that this scripture must be fulfilled in me, 'And he was reckoned with transgressors'" (22:27).

Luke has already made clear to his readers that beneath the hostility of the leaders there lurks another source of evil and hatred. The violation of Jesus' freedom and his march to death were not simply a miscarriage of justice by misguided human beings. A more important actor had entered the stage of the passion: "This is your hour and *the power of darkness*" (22:53). The drama beginning to unfold was the ultimate struggle between life and death, between the power of God and the de-humanizing power of Evil.[23]

---

[22]See above pp. 44-46; On Luke's more positive treatment of the *laos* or "people" see J. Crowe, "The *Laos* at the Cross," in A. Lacomara (ed.), *The Language of the Cross* (Chicago: Franciscan Herald Press, 1977), 77-101.

[23]Luke uses the image of "darkness" here, as he had in 11:35, "Therefore be careful lest the light in you be darkness." Even more significant are Paul's words to Agrippa in Acts 26:17-18 where he recounts his conversion experience. The Risen

Although the violence about to be inflicted on Jesus might appear as a triumph of "darkness," the reader knows that the light of Jesus will not be snuffed out. Luke asserts this even as the arrest takes place. Only when Jesus has finished speaking can the leaders seize him (22:54 "*Then* they seized him).... And Luke will make no mention of the flight of the disciples so prominent in the accounts of Mark (14:50-51) and Matthew (26:56). The evangelist is silent about this because he has already stated that Jesus' powerful prayer for their perseverance would repulse Satan's designs on them (22:28-32). They would be convulsed with fear and stay to the periphery of events during the Passion, and Peter himself would go to the brink of apostasy. But ultimately God's light would dispel the darkness.

IV. In the House of the High Priest: Denial (22:54-62) and Mockery (22:63-65).

Once Jesus has been arrested, the pace of the story quickens. He is taken to the house of the High Priest, the setting for the two scenes that follow.

> [54]Then they seized him and led him away, bringing him into the high priest's house. Peter followed at a distance; [55]and when they had kindled a fire in the middle of the courtyard and sat down together, Peter sat among them. [56]Then a maid seeing him as he sat in the light and gazing at him, said, "This man also was with him." [57]But he denied it, saying, "Woman, I do not know him." [58]And a little later some one else saw him and said, "You also are one of them." But Peter said, "Man, I am not." [59]And after an interval of about an hour still another insisted, saying, "Certainly this man also was with him; for he is a Galilean." [60]But Peter said, "Man, I do not know what you are saying." And immediately, while he was still speak-

Christ had sent him "to open their (the Gentiles') eyes that they may turn from darkness to light and from the power of Satan to God...."

ing, the cock crowed. [61]And the Lord turned and looked at Peter. And Peter remembered the word of the Lord, how he had said to him, "Before the cock crows today, you will deny me three times." [62]And he went out and wept bitterly.

[63]Now the men who were holding Jesus mocked him and beat him; [64]they also blindfolded him and asked him, "Prophesy! Who is it that struck you?" [65]And they spoke many other words against him, reviling him.

Luke departs from the sequence of events found in his major source, Mark. In the latter's account, Peter's threefold denial (Mk 14:53-54, 66-72) surrounds Jesus' nighttime interrogation by the Sanhedrin (14:55-65).[1] Thereby Peter's denial of his identity as a disciple contrasts sharply with Jesus' courageous confession of his identity as Messiah. Then after the night session and Jesus' mockery (14:65), the Sanhedrin gathers in the early morning to hold another consultation before bringing Jesus to Pilate (15:1).

The sequence and setting of the Lukan account are different. The full account of Peter's denial is narrated immediately, before Jesus' interrogation. In effect, Luke links the Peter episode more tightly with the *previous* scenes about the need for prayer in the face of test. The prediction Jesus made at the passover meal about Peter being "sifted like wheat" (22:31) is now fulfilled. Luke also eliminates the nighttime session of the Sanhedrin. Jesus' night of captivity is filled with mockery and torture. Both Peter's denial and the mockery take place in the house of the high priest (22:54)[2] Only at daybreak is Jesus brought before the Sanhedrin for questioning (22:66).[3]

---

[1]See D. Senior, *The Passion of Jesus in the Gospel of Mark*, 87-88. Matthew follows Mark's sequence.

[2]This is similar to the double setting in John's Gospel in which Jesus is first taken to the house of Annas (John 18:13) where the first of Peter's denials takes place (18:15-18), and later to the house of Caiaphas the high priest (18:24).

[3]In the view of many scholars, Luke's version of a morning rather than a night trial appears to be more historically probable. The legality of a nightime trial under Jewish law is questionable. However, it is very difficult to determine what precisely

The overall effect of Luke's presentation is to put the spotlight on these two terrible moments of the Passion. They are not episodes submerged in the trial or interrogation before the Sanhedrin. Both Peter's cowardly denial of his discipleship and the mockery and torture rained on Jesus confirm his warnings about the impending test. Some interpreters contend that Luke must have used a separate non-Markan source in his construction of these scenes, but his freewheeling editing of Mark seems a more likely explanation.

A) PETER'S DENIAL (22:54-65).

Luke concluded the arrest scene without mentioning the disciples.[4] But once Jesus is seized and led to the high priest's house, we learn that Peter is still present, "follow(ing) at a distance" (22:54). Jesus' prediction about Satan's vicious attempt to break Peter is still fresh in the reader's memory (22:31). So, too, is Jesus' own struggle in prayer to be ready for combat, and the disciples' weakness, as they do not pray but succumb to fear and sleep (22:45-56). With this preparation, it is clear that Luke considers Peter's denials a weak and nearly tragic response to Satan's test.

---

was Jewish law on this point in the first third of the first century, or to be conclusive on how faithful the leaders were to this procedure in a given situation. Even if it could be established that a night trial was illegal and improbable historically, it is not certain that Luke's presentation differs from Mark's because of sensitivity to this historical issue. For further discussion, see J. Fitzmyer, *The Gospel According to Luke X-XXIV*, 1453-63. On the Markan version, see D. Senior, *The Passion of Jesus in the Gospel of Mark*, 88-90. Matthew follows Mark in presenting a night interrogation by the Sanhedrin (26:57-68) but reserves their formal condemnation of Jesus until the morning session (see 27:1); see, D. Senior, *The Passion of Jesus in the Gospel of Matthew*, 103.

[4]It is interesting to observe Luke's caution *vis a vis* the Markan tradition here. Although Luke wishes to emphasize the ultimate perseverance of the disciples (see above, 22:28) he cannot directly contradict the tradition about their flight at the moment of the arrest, a point so forcefully made in Mark (14:50-51, including the flight of one disciple naked!) and Matthew (26:56). Thus Luke remains silent about the presence of the disciples when Jesus is arrested; later in the Passion story he will suggest their presence at the perimeter of the action; see below, 23:49, and S. Brown, *Apostasy and Perseverance*, 67-68.

Luke is subtle in his preparation for the scene. Unlike Mark where the fire kindled in the courtyard *warms* Peter (Mk 14:54), in Luke the fire *throws light* on Peter (22:56). As Peter "sat in the light" a maid servant recognizes him. Does Luke intend anything more by this detail than simply a setting for the scene? Or is the image of darkness and light evoked at the arrest scene still in play? There Jesus had told his captors that it was their "hour" and "the power of darkness" (22:53). Now darkness envelops the scene, but Peter sits "in the light" where his bond with Jesus becomes evident to the bystanders. The warning of Jesus echoes hauntingly in the background: "Therefore be careful lest the light in you be darkness..." (11:35).

Three times Peter is confronted. The first is a maid who "gazes" at Peter, recognizing him and accusing him of being "with him" (22:56). Peter's denial of his bond with Jesus is complete: "I do not know him" (22:57). This is more sharply put than in Mark's parallel where Peter's first response is an attempted diversion, "I neither know nor understand what you mean" (Mk 14:68). The next two accusations are by men; some commentators wonder if Luke is conscious here of Jewish law whereby serious accusations must be confirmed by two male witnesses (see Deut 19:15).[5] More important is the vehemence of Peter's denials. The second accuser shifts the attention to Peter's association with the disciples: "You also are one of *them*"; but again he flatly denies it (22:58). The third accuser returns to Peter's bond with Jesus: "Certainly this man also was *with him*; for he is a Galilean" (22:59). This time Peter feigns ignorance, "Man, I do not know what you are saying."

For fear of exposure, Peter denies his relationship to Jesus and to his fellow disciples. Both relationships are key for Peter's role in Luke-Acts. Peter was the first disciple called by Jesus and the first to be commissioned as a "catcher of

---

[5]See, J. Fitzmyer, *The Gospel According to Luke X-XXIV*, 1460; J. Ford, *My Enemy is my Guest,* 122; I.H. Marshall, *Commentary on Luke*, 839; F. Matera, *Passion Narratives and Gospel Theologies,* 171.

people" (see Luke 5:1-11). At the passover meal he was entrusted with the mission of "strengthening" the other disciples. In Acts, Peter would take the lead in reconstituting the twelve (Acts 1:15-26) and would be the first to proclaim the message of the Risen Christ after Pentecost (Acts 2:14-22). Even the accuser's reference to Peter's "Galilean" origin has special poignancy in this Gospel; Galilee was the place where Jesus' mission had begun and where he had first called his disciples. Peter's denials cut across all of these bonds, threatening the very foundation of his identity as a disciple of Jesus.

Luke draws attention to the lapse of time as the denials unfold—"after an interval of about an hour" (22:59). The clock is ticking off the moments until the fulfillment of the prophecy Jesus made at the passover meal: "I tell you, Peter, the cock will crow this day, until you three times deny that you know me" (22:34). Luke has this prophecy come true as the third denial is still on Peter's lips ("...immediately, while he was still speaking..." 22:60). The cock crow pierces the night air.

In Mark and Matthew's accounts the sound of cockcrow jostles Peter's memory and reminds him of what Jesus had said (see Mk 14:72; Mt 26:75). Luke introduces a significant new element: Jesus turns and looks at Peter (22:61). In his staging of the scene Luke has placed both Jesus and Peter in the same courtyard.[6] That silent look between the captive master and frightened disciple breaks through Peter's cowardice, reestablishing the bond of love he had trampled. *Then* Peter remembers "the word of the Lord," warning him of the impending test so severe that it would lead Peter himself to the brink of apostasy. The realization of his sin cuts to Peter's heart and he weeps tears of repentance (22:62).

There is little doubt that Luke considered this scene an important instruction on discipleship. Its basic thrust is similar to the scene at the passover meal. There, too, Luke blends

---

[6]M. Soards, "'And The Lord Turned and Looked Straight at Peter': Understanding Luke 22, 61," *Biblica* 67 (1986) 518-19.

images of the disciples' startling weakness with Jesus' tenacious and ultimately redeeming love for them.[7]

B) THE MOCKERY OF THE PROPHET (22:63-65).

A brief but terrible scene concludes the episodes in the house of the high priest. The "men who were holding Jesus" begin to mock and beat him (22:63). Luke's sequence of events gives a special shade of meaning to this scene. In Mark and Matthew the mockery comes as a conclusion of the trial in which the Sanhedrin condemns Jesus for blasphemy because of his claim to be Son of God. But in Luke the mockery *precedes* the interrogation and is more closely connected with the previous string of events. Peter's denial of Jesus had confirmed his prophetic warnings at the passover meal about the rigors of the test that lay ahead. Now Jesus' captors mock him for pretending to be a prophet, an act of violence that ironically enables the reader to witness the fulfillment of Jesus' prophetic powers.

The captors blindfold him and demand that he "prophesy" and name his tormentors (22:64). The abuse hurled at Jesus simply confirms his identity as prophet. Right from the start of Jesus' mission, Luke stresses that rejection and suffering were the lot of the prophets sent to Israel.[8] In the synagogue of Nazareth, Jesus quoted the proverb that "no prophet is acceptable in his own country" (4:24). The fate of Israel's rejected prophets is recalled and a similar destiny predicted for those who follow Jesus (6:22-23; 11:47-51; 13:33-35; 20:9-18). When forecasting his own passion, Jesus had included a prediction of "mockery" and "shameful treatment" (18:32).

The grip of the "power of darkness" tightens. Jesus experiences denial by his own followers and now mockery and torture from his own people. The final rejection by the leaders is about to take place.

---

[7]See above, discussion of 22:24-38.

[8]See above, Part I, pp. 28-31.

V. Rejection by the Leaders of Israel: Jesus before the Sanhedrin (22:66-71).

The setting of the Passion drama shifts once more, as daylight breaks and Jesus is taken from the high priest's house to the full council of the Jewish leaders:

> 66When day came, the assembly of the elders of the people gathered together, both chief priests and scribes; and they led him away to their council, and they said, 67"If you are the Christ, tell us." But he said to them, "If I tell you, you will not believe; 68and if I ask you, you will not answer. 69But from now on the Son of man shall be seated at the right hand of the power of God." 70And they all said, "Are you the Son of God, then?" And he said to them, "You say that I am." 71And they said, "What further testimony do we need? We have heard it ourselves from his own lips."

As he has throughout the Passion story, Luke reworks the account of Mark to highlight certain themes important to his Gospel. In the previous two scenes, the evangelist had emphasized simultaneously Jesus' clear identity as God's Spirit-filled prophet and the rejection of that claim by others. Peter's denial had validated Jesus' warnings at the passover meal, at the same time that the disciple's failure added to Jesus' sufferings. Those who held him captive mocked Jesus' supposed pretensions to be a prophet and, ironically, confirmed his vocation as a prophet who suffers rejection by God's people.

Luke continues and intensifies the motif of rejection in this scene. He screens from Mark's account other considerations such as the false testimony concerning Jesus' threats against the temple (see Mk 14:56-59). Luke is aware of this material since it appears as part of the leaders' accusations against Stephen in Acts: "...for we have heard him say that this Jesus of Nazareth will destroy this place (the temple), and will change the customs which Moses delivered to us" (Acts 6:14). But here in the Passion story Luke does not swerve in this direction. This may be partly due to Luke's reverence for the Jerusalem temple; he is more positive about Jerusalem and its temple than the other evangelists.[1] But even more important is the evangelist's concentration on the central issue of Jesus' identity and the rejection of him by the Sanhedrin.

He carefully sets the scene for this single, morning gathering of the Council. The whole assembly of "the elders of the people . . . both chief priests and scribes" (22:66) come together for a formal hearing. This council, or Sanhedrin, does not end with an official verdict; in this, Luke differs from Mark (14:64) and Matthew (27:1).[2] Luke seems to present this meeting of the council as a hearing or interrogation which ends with a rejection of Jesus as Messiah and Son of God. Formal judicial condemnation is reserved for the trial before Pilate.

Luke's interest is clear in the forceful dialogue that takes place at this hearing. There is no stream of witnesses; the action moves immediately to the exchange between Jesus and the leaders. The key questions are posed not by the high priest alone but by the entire assembly (22:67, 70), an awkward staging, except that Luke wants this to be the collective statement of the leaders. Jesus does not remain silent through most of the proceedings but directly challenges his questioners (22:67-68; contrast Mk 14:61). Again in contrast to Mark and Matthew who combine key titles of "Christ" and "Son of God" in a single question (Mk 14:61; Mt 26:63), Luke separates them into two dramatic challenges to Jesus' mission.

The council first asks: "If you are the Christ, tell us"

---

[1] The Gospel begins (1:8-9) and ends (24:53) in the Temple. In Acts the post-Easter Jerusalem community will continue to pray in the temple and perform miracles there. On Luke's attitude to the temple, see F.D. Weinert, "The Meaning of the Temple in Luke-Acts," *Biblical Theology Bulletin* 11 (1981) 85-89; "Luke, Stephen and the Temple in Luke-Acts," *Biblical Theology Bulletin* 17 (1987) 88-91; J. Tyson, *The Death of Jesus in Luke-Acts*, 84-113.

[2] In Mark this verdict is reached at the conclusion of the night trial (Mk 14:64). Matthew, perhaps sensitive to the law on this point, reserves it for their morning gathering (27:1). See above, p. 94, n. 3,

(22:67). The disbelieving tone of this question is betrayed by the conditional, "*if you are . . .*". Satan had begun his testing of Jesus in the desert in the same manner (4:3,9). And the mockers at the cross would pose their taunts with similar words: "*if he is* the Christ of God . . . " (23:35), "*If you are* the King of the Jews. . ." (23:37). Jesus' sharp reply confirms that the council's question is tantamount to rejecting him as the Christ: "If I tell you, you will not believe; and if I ask you, you will not answer" (22:67-68). These words are reminiscent of the impasse Jesus had reached with the leaders when he taught in the temple and when their hostility to him had reached the boiling point. Truth and openness had become victims of the leaders' determination to destroy Jesus, as a result they could no longer dare to respond to him (see 20:3-8, 19-26, 40). Jesus could no longer speak to them, nor could he question or challenge them. From this Gospel's perspective, in which the word of Jesus was powerful and redemptive, no more chilling condemnation could be imagined.[3]

In spite of their intransigence, Jesus goes on to respond to the leaders' question. "From now on the Son of Man shall be seated at the right hand of the power of God" (22:69). The council had asked about Jesus' identity as the "Christ" or messiah. Jesus responds in terms of the "Son of Man." As do all the evangelists, Luke uses this mysterious title to describe important aspects of Jesus' mission.[4] Although Luke cites it

[3]Luke stresses the power of Jesus' word, often referring to his preaching as "the word of God": see, for example, Lk 5:1; 8:11, 21; 11:28. In Acts the community's own preaching is also described with this same phrase, thereby linking it to the preaching of Jesus: see Acts 4:31; 6:2, 7; 8:14; 11:1; 12:24; 13:5, 7, 44, 46, 48; 16:32; 17:13; 18:11. On this point, see J. Fitzmyer, *The Gospel According to Luke I-X* 565; J. Kodell, "The Word of God Grew: The Ecclesial Tendency of *Logos* in Acts 1:7; 12:24; 19:20," *Biblica* 55 (1974) 505-19; R. O'Toole, *The Unity of Luke-Acts*, 86-94.

[4]The Aramaic term *bar 'enash* at the root of this title can mean simply a generic designation for a "human being." It is possible that it is used in this generic way in Daniel 7:13, "I saw in the night visions, and behold, with the clouds of heaven there came one like a *son of man*, and he came to the Ancient of Days and was presented before him." In the Gospels the term appears consistently on the lips of Jesus himself. Jesus may also have used the phrase in this same non-titular manner to refer indirectly to himself. However, some scholars contend that even in Daniel this phrase is already used in a titular sense to refer to a collective triumphant Israel. In

in connection with Jesus' ministry of forgiving sins (5:24) and healing (6:5; 19:10), he applies it most to two crucial, and paradoxically related, aspects of Jesus' messianic destiny: his humiliation and rejection, and his triumphant exaltation and glorious return.[5]

Both of those dimensions are present as Jesus faces the Sanhedrin. He is the humiliated and rejected Son of Man as he stands beaten, mocked, and accused before the leaders. But his bold answer proclaims his exaltation: "From now on the Son of man shall be seated at the right hand of the power of God" (22:69). This reply has subtle differences from that given in Mark and Matthew. Similar to them, Jesus' words are a blend of Daniel 7:13 and Psalm 110:1.[6] But Luke concentrates on affirming Jesus' exaltation, omitting reference to the "coming with the clouds of heaven" and the leaders' "seeing" of the Son of Man. These latter elements emphasize the parousia when the Son of Man would come in judgment. But in Luke, Jesus proclaims his triumph over rejection and death: as the victorious Son of Man he will be "seated at the right hand of the power of God." This glorious end has been in view from the very beginning of the Gospel. When Jesus is attacked at Nazareth, he passes through their midst and goes on his way (4:30). That way leads to God (9:31, 51). The Christ "must suffer" but he will also be vindicated by God and raised from the dead (24:46). The ascension is Luke's way of affirming this glorious victory of Jesus over death. The crucified and Risen Christ is carried up to heaven in triumph, his mission completed (Lk 24:50-53; Acts 1:9-11).

later Jewish and New Testament texts, the phrase definitely takes on titular meaning now applied to an individual. On this see, F. Hahn, *The Titles of Jesus in Christology*, (London: Lutterworth, 15-53); J. Dunn, *Christology in the Making* (Philadelphia: Westminister, 1980), 65-97; B. Lindars, *Jesus Son of Man* (Grand Rapids: Eerdmans, 1984); J. Fitzmyer, *The Gospel According to Luke I-X*, 208-11.

[5]Rejection: see 6:22; 7:34; 9:22, 26, 44, 58; 18:31-33; exaltation: 12:8, 10; future coming: 12:40; 17:22, 23, 26, 30; 18:8; 21:27.

[6]"I saw in the night visions, and behold, with the clouds of heaven there came one like a son of man, and he came to the Ancient of Days and was presented before him" (Daniel 7:13).
"The Lord says to my lord: 'Sit at my right hand, till I make your enemies your footstool.'" (Psalm 110:1).

In his Pentecost sermon Peter proclaims the same message, drawing on Psalm 110 in words strongly reminiscent of the trial scene:

> "This Jesus God raised up, and of that we all are witnesses. Being therefore exalted at the right hand of God, and having received from the Father the promise of the Holy Spirit, he has poured out this which you see and hear. For David did not ascend into the heavens; but he himself says, 'The Lord said to my Lord, Sit at my right hand, till I make thy enemies a stool for thy feet.' Let all the house of Israel therefore know assuredly that God has made him both Lord and Christ, this Jesus whom you crucified." (Acts 2:32-36)

The martyr Stephen would confirm Jesus' victory as death closes in on him and he sees a vision of the triumphant Jesus: "But he, full of the Holy Spirit, gazed into heaven and saw the glory of God, and Jesus standing at the right hand of God; and he said, 'Behold, I see the heavens opened, and the Son of man standing at the right hand of God.'" (Acts 7:55-56).

In response to the Sanhedrin's question about his messianic identity, Jesus evokes the full scope of his God-given destiny. The messiah is the Son of Man who must suffer rejection and even death in the course of his liberating mission. But God will vindicate the Christ, raising him from death and exalting him to a share in God's own power.

The second question keys on another major title for Jesus: "Are you the *Son of God*, then?" (22:70). By separating it from the "Christ" title in the council's questions, Luke indicates that the two titles are not identical in meaning.[7] "Son of God" points to Jesus' unique relationship to God. The message of Gabriel to Mary at the very beginning of the Gospel states this clearly: "The Holy Spirit will come upon

---

[7]See J. Fitzmyer, *The Gospel of Luke I-X*, 205-208; G. Schneider, *Verleugnung, Verspottung und Verhor Jesu Nach Lukas 22, 54-71* (München: Kosel, 1969), 172-74.

you, and the power of the Most High will overshadow you; therefore the child to be born will be called holy, the Son of God" (1:35). Luke's genealogy tracks Jesus' origins back through the figures of salvation history, back through Adam the Father of the human race, back to God (3:38). There, mysteriously bonded with God, is Jesus' ultimate beginning and end. God's voice declared it so at the baptism (3:22) and again at the transfiguration (9:35). Jesus himself was moved by the Holy Spirit to exult in that love between father and son, "All things have been delivered to me by my Father; and no one knows who the Son is except the Father, or who the Father is except the Son and any one to whom the Son chooses to reveal him" (10:22-23).

Whereas the "Christ" or Messiah title reveals Jesus' role as liberating redeemer of God's people, "Son of God" points to Jesus' mysterious communion with God, the ultimate source of his authority and power. That communion would be tested and found strong in the events of the Passion.

The Sanhedrin's own question has ironically stated the truth about Jesus: "You, therefore, are the Son of God?" Jesus' answer confirms that the truth has come from their own lips: "You say that I am."[8] But the Sanhedrin is set on rejecting Jesus; they cannot accept that he is the Christ, or the Son of God. There is no need for "further testimony" because Jesus himself has fearlessly declared who he is (22:71). The contrast with Peter's cowardly denial of his identity is inescapable. Jesus had warned the disciples that they would experience persecution in which they would be "deliver(ed) up to the synagogues and prisons, and ... brought before kings and governors for my name's sake. This will be a time for you to bear testimony." (21:12-13). The word "testimony" or "witness" (*marturion*) used here is the same as in 22:71. Jesus himself gives a perfect example of what he had encouraged his disciples to do. Dragged before

---

[8]It is inconceivable that the Lukan Jesus would reject this title already given to him repeatedly in the Gospel. The formula "you say that I am" is similar to the statements in Mt 26:25, 64 and 27:11 which confirm the truth of what the questioner poses; see D. Senior, *The Passion of Jesus in the Gospel of Matthew*, 64.

a court because of his mission, he fearlessly gives witness.

As the hearing before the Sanhedrin concludes, the power of darkness seems to have the upper hand. The leaders reject Jesus as Messiah and Son of God. But even in this somber moment, the prophet-martyr gives an example of deliberate courage. Jesus does not flinch before his enemies or attempt to mask the truth. He is the Christ, the Son of God, and his triumph over death will be complete.

VI. The Trial: Interrogation by Pilate (23:1-5), Displayed before Herod (23:6-12), Condemnation (23:13-25).

The members of the Sanhedrin take Jesus from their meeting hall to Pilate the Roman governor. This change of scene ushers in a major part of the Passion drama: Jesus on trial. Three episodes make up this part of the narrative: Pilate's initial interrogation of Jesus (23:1-5), the encounter with Herod (23:6-12), and the final condemnation of Jesus (23:13-25).

> [1]Then the whole company of them arose, and brought him before Pilate. [2]And they began to accuse him, saying, "We found this man perverting our nation, and forbidding us to give tribute to Caesar, and saying that he himself is Christ a king." [3]And Pilate asked him, "Are you the King of the Jews?" And he answered him, "You have said so." [4]And Pilate said to the chief priests and the multitudes, "I find no crime in this man." [5]But they were urgent, saying, "He stirs up the people, teaching throughout all Judea, from Galilee even to this place."
> [6]When Pilate heard this, he asked whether the man was a Galilean. [7]And when he learned that he belonged to Herod's jurisdiction, he sent him over to Herod, who was himself in Jerusalem at that time. [8]When Herod saw Jesus, he was very glad, for he had long desired to see him, because he had heard about him, and he was hoping to see some sign done by him. [9]So he questioned him at

some length; but he made no answer. [10]The chief priests and the scribes stood by, vehemently accusing him. [11]And Herod with his soldiers treated him with contempt and mocked him; then, arraying him in gorgeous apparel, he sent him back to Pilate. [12]And Herod and Pilate became friends with each other that very day, for before this they had been at enmity with each other.

[13]Pilate then called together the chief priests and the rulers and the people, [14]and said to them, "You brought me this man as one who was perverting the people; and after examining him before you, behold, I did not find this man guilty of any of your charges against him; [15]neither did Herod, for he sent him back to us. Behold, nothing deserving death has been done by him; [16]I will therefore chastise him and release him." [17]Now he was obliged to release one man to them at the festival.

[18]But they all cried out together, "Away with this man, and release to us Barabbas"—[19]a man who had been thrown into prison for an insurrection started in the city, and for murder. [20]Pilate addressed them once more, desiring to release Jesus; [21]but they shouted out, "Crucify him!" [22]A third time he said to them, "Why, what evil has he done? I have found in him no crime deserving death; I will therefore chastise him and release him." [23]But they were urgent, demanding with loud cries that he should be crucified. And their voices prevailed.

[24]So Pilate gave sentence that their demand should be granted. [25]He released the man who had been thrown into prison for insurrection and murder, whom they asked for; but Jesus he delivered up to their will.

A) INTERROGATION BY PILATE (23:1-5)

The terrible moment predicted by Jesus now comes true: "For (the Son of man) will be delivered to the Gentiles" (18:32). Luke stresses the initiative of the leaders in handing over Jesus to the Romans. The "whole company of them," that is, the leaders who had just rejected Jesus' testimony (22:71) "stand up" as a single body and lead their prisoner to

Pilate. Luke maintains a strong connection with the previous events by continuing to demonstrate the leaders' rejection of Jesus. But the tension in the drama rachets upward because Pilate has the power to put Jesus to death. And for the first time "the crowds" will join the leaders in seeking to destroy Jesus (23:4).

In this first encounter with Pilate, the leaders bring forward a series of formal charges against Jesus. In contrast to the hearing before the Sanhedrin, the four charges stated are strongly political in nature: (1) Jesus "perverts our nation" (23:2); (2) he "forbids us to give tribute to Caesar" (23:2); (3) he claims he is "Christ a king" (23:2); and (4) he "stirs up the people, teaching throughout all Judea, from Galilee even to this place" (23:5).

It is difficult to determine exactly what Luke intended by having such an obvious contrast between the accusations before the Sanhedrin and those before Pilate. There is some historical logic in Luke's account: while the Jewish Sanhedrin would be concerned primarily with Jesus' religious claims, the Romans would care only about political charges, especially those bordering on sedition, as all four of these do. But Luke's main purpose may be theological rather than historical. The evangelist wanted to demonstrate that the entire proceedings against Jesus were unjust.[1] The religious leaders obviously trumped up these charges to have Jesus condemned by the Romans. But neither Pilate nor Herod found Jesus guilty of them. Building on this last point, some commentators suggest that Luke's primary purpose was to show that Roman society had nothing to fear from the Christian movement. Even though Jesus was crucified, the charges of sedition against him were unfounded. The Roman procurator who condemned him had repeatedly declared his innocence; the unjust accusations of the Jewish leaders and

---

[1]See, for example, J. Tyson, *The Death of Jesus in Luke-Acts*, p. 129; I.H. Marshall, *Commentary on Luke*, 852; E. LaVerdiere, *Luke* (New Testament Message 5; Wilmington: Michael Glazier, 1980), 272-73; G. Schneider, "The Political Charge Against Jesus (Luke 23:2)," in E. Bammel and C.F.D. Moule (eds.), *Jesus and the Politics of His Day*, 403-14.

mob pressure brought about his crucifixion.[2]

In fact all three of these factors may be in play to some degree. But whether Luke wishes to portray Jesus as totally "innocent" of these charges and is intent only on reassuring the Romans that Christianity is harmless is another matter.[3] Some clarity may come in a closer look at the details of the scene.

The leaders begin the trial by hurling three charges against Jesus. Luke seems to build on Mark's account where the accusations against Jesus are assumed but not stated (see Mk 15:1-2).[4] The first charge, "perverting our nation, " is quite general. The Greek word *diastrephonta* literally means to "make crooked." Ironically, Jesus had used this term himself when confronted with the inability of his disciples to cure a possessed boy: "O faithless and *perverse (diestram-mene)* generation. . . " (9:41). In Acts, Simon Magus is condemned for attempting to "pervert" (*diastrepsai*) the faith of the proconsul Sergius Paulus (13:8, 10). And in his speech to the elders of the Ephesian church, Paul warns them of false teachers who will arise "speaking *perverse (diestrammena)* things, to draw away the disciples after them" (Acts 20:30). To "pervert the nation," therefore, implies that Jesus had been leading the people astray. The leaders do not refer to specific incidents in the Gospel story, but the reader is conscious of the tide of opposition generated by Jesus' prophetic teaching and ministry.[5] The reader of the Gospel knows that Jesus' teaching is not "perverse" but, at the same time, is equally aware that his words and actions were meant to

---

[2]See P. Walasky, "The Trial and Death of Jesus in the Gospel of Luke," *Journal of Biblical Literature* 94 (1975) 81-85; J. Massyngbaerde Ford, *My Enemy is My Guest*, 124-27.

[3]On this important distinction, see the discussion in R. Cassidy, *Jesus, Politics, and Society* (Maryknoll: Orbis, 1978), 63-86; also D. Schmidt, "Luke's 'Innocent' Jesus: A Scriptural Apologetic," in R. Cassidy & P. Scharper, *Political Issues in Luke-Acts*, 111-21.

[4]In both Mark (15:2) and Matthew (27:11), the scene begins with Pilate's question: "Are you the King of the Jews?"—no accusations lead into the governor's question.

[5]See above, Part I, pp. 21-23.

radically change God's people and to turn them in a new direction.

The second accusation is quite specific: "forbidding us to give tribute to Caesar." The connection to an earlier incident in the Gospel is evident. During Jesus' final days of teaching in the temple, the scribes and chief priests had sent spies to trap Jesus "so as to deliver him up to the authority and jurisdiction of the governor" (20:20). The question about paying taxes to Caesar was meant to trip him up. The famous answer, "Then render to Caesar the things that are Caesar's, and to God the things that are God's," stuns Jesus' enemies; "they were not able in the presence of the people to catch him by what he said; but marveling at his answer they were silent" (20:26). This conclusion to the scene shows that Luke did not interpret Jesus' somewhat enigmatic answer as an outright refusal to pay taxes. So the charge in the trial is false. At the same time, Jesus' teaching about "render to God the things that are God's" also claims a higher and all-pervasive allegiance that leaves in doubt Caesar's claims to sovereignty.[6] Thus here, too, the accusation at the trial, while patently false on the surface, contains an ironic truth about Jesus' teaching.

This dual level of meaning is most clear regarding the third accusation, that Jesus claims he is "Christ a King." In this context, the leaders obviously mean that Jesus was claiming to be a political king, challenging Roman authority.[7] As such it is a false charge. And one could say that there is no evidence in the Gospel that Jesus proclaimed himself to be

[6]See, J. Duncan M. Derrett, "Luke's Perspective on Tribute to Caesar," in R. Cassidy & P. Scharper (eds.), *Political Issues in Luke-Acts*, 38-48; and the review of interpretations in J. Fitzmyer, *The Gospel According to Luke X-XXIV*, 1289-94.

[7]A similar accusation is made in Acts 17:7-9 against Jason and some of the other Christians at Thessalonica in the wake of Paul's ministry there: "'These men who have turned the world upside down have come here also, and Jason has received them; and they are all acting against the decrees of Caesar, saying that there is another king, Jesus.' And the people and the city were disturbed when they heard this."

110 *The Passion of Jesus*

the messiah. In Luke that title is offered to Jesus by others but never by himself.[8]

But on another level the Gospel does not hesitate to portray Jesus as the royal Davidic messiah, as God's anointed king. This is evident in scenes from the Passion itself, as in the hearing before the Sanhedrin where Jesus does not deny his kingship (22:67-69), or at the passover meal where he speaks of "my kingdom" and appoints the apostles as judges over the twelve tribes of Israel (22:30).[9] This motif, too, has strong preparation earlier in the Gospel. Jesus is proclaimed king in the infancy gospel: "...the Lord God will give to him the throne of his father David, and he will reign over the house of Jacob for ever; and of his kingdom there will be no end" (1:32-33). Proclamation of the kingdom is the stated theme of Jesus' ministry (4:43). And while cautioning his disciples not to make it public, Jesus accepts Peter's acclamation, "the Christ of God" (9:20).

The climax of all this comes as Jesus enters Jerusalem. Luke's version of this scene makes it an unabashed royal procession (19:28-40). As he draws near Jerusalem his disciples exult, "Blessed is the King who comes in the name of the Lord! Peace in heaven and glory in the highest!" The Pharisees are shocked at this and ask Jesus to silence his disciples but he answers, "I tell you, if these were silent, the very stones would cry out" (19:40).

Thus Luke has made no secret of Jesus' royal identity. He is "Christ a king," one whose presence creates turbulence. While the leaders' accusation is crudely false on one level, it is ironically and decisively true on another.

Jesus' alleged claim to political power—the real basis of all the others—is the only accusation to which Pilate reacts. He asks Jesus directly, "Are you the King of the Jews?" (23:3). Jesus' response, "You have said so," is identical to that found in Mark's version (Mk 15:2). Its tone—confirming

[8]For example, 2:11 (an Angel of the Lord), 4:41 (the people); 9:20 (Peter).

[9]There are also important references to the advent of the Kingdom in 22:16, 18; see above, pp. 56-58.

that the words are those of the accusers not his own—fits perfectly into the irony at play in Luke's scene. Jesus *is* a king (hence he does not deny the charge) but *not* in the manner his accusers think (hence he stops short of a straight acceptance of the charge).

Pilate's declaration of innocence, the first of three in the trial scene (see 23:13-14, 22), comes abruptly, without elaboration: "I find no crime in this man" (23:4).[10] He addresses the chief priests and "the multitudes" (literally, "the crowds", *ochlous*). This is the first time the "crowds" are mentioned in the trial scene. As noted above, the "crowds" are generally favorable to Jesus in Luke's Gospel, sometimes in explicit contrast to the hostility of the leaders.[11] Later in this scene the "people" (*ho laos*) will play a significant role (see below, 23:13-25), but for the moment their attitude is undefined.

Pilate's conclusion is unacceptable to Jesus' opponents. "They" (Are the "crowds" included at this point?) urgently bring forward another charge in order to stave off Jesus' release (23:5). Here again Luke seems to be highlighting the bad faith of Jesus' enemies. The charge itself is rather generic, similar to the that of "perverting the nation" at the beginning of the trial: "He stirs up the people, teaching throughout all Judea, from Galilee even to this place" (23:5). The dual level of meaning present in all of the accusations is also present here. As an accusation of purely political sedition it is false. But on a deeper, ironic, level, it is a true summary of Jesus' entire ministry. His teaching *had* "stirred up the people" (here Luke uses the collective term, *ho laos*), as Luke's story frequently reported.[12] And the scope of that mission had involved a fateful journey throughout the entire land of Israel, from Galilee "even to this place." Here Luke has the accusers describe Jesus' ministry in his own favored terms, as an all-encompassing journey from Galilee to Jerusalem ("this

[10]The Greek wording is quite emphatic, beginning with the word "nothing," literally: "Nothing have I found worthy (of condemnation) in this man."

[11]See above, 22:6.

[12]See, for example, 4:14-15, 31-32; 5:1; 6:17-19; 7:29; 18:43; 19:48, etc.

place").[13] The mention of "Galilee" also provides the clue for the next scene in which Jesus is brought to another hearing, this time before the Galilean ruler, Herod.

Throughout this opening episode of the trial, Luke maintains his fundamental perspective on the Passion. Although surrounded by the power of darkness, God's Son and prophet is triumphant. For those who hear this story with faith, even the desperate accusations of his enemies cannot suppress the truth about Jesus. And the very Roman Governor who will condemn him to death declares that Jesus is without guilt.

B) BROUGHT BEFORE HEROD (23:6-12).

A curious interlude in the trial now takes place. When Pilate learns from the Jewish leaders that Jesus is from Galilee (23:5-6), he sends the prisoner to Herod Antipas, the tetrarch of Galilee who would have jurisdiction over Jesus in his home region. Herod was in Jerusalem—part of Judea which was under direct Roman rule—for the feast of passover.

There is considerable debate about the historical plausibility of this scene. Some believe that Luke must have had a special historical tradition for such an incident,[14] while others suggest that Luke himself elaborates the incident for theological and dramatic purposes.[15] What concerns us here is how

[13]J. Tyson suggests that, given the wider context of 19:45-21:38 where Jesus was teaching in the temple, "this place" refers not only to Jerusalem but to the temple itself (*The Death of Jesus in Luke-Acts*, 109). But the immediate context holds greater weight here and it is scarcely possible that the leaders refer to the temple as "this place" when they are standing before Pilate. On the journey narrative in Luke, see above, Part I, pp. 35-39.

[14]See, for example, I. Howard Marshall, *Commentary on Luke*, 854-55.

[15]J. Neyrey, for example, argues that all of the elements in the Herod story have a foundation in either the Gospel of Mark (e.g., 6:14-16), or in Lukan redactional additions to Mark (e.g., Lk. 9:9), or in Luke's concern with scriptural fulfillment; see, *The Passion According to Luke*, 77-80. A thorough discussion of the source question is also found in J. Fitzmyer, *The Gospel According to Luke X-XXIV*, 1478-80; M. Soards, "Tradition, Composition and Theology in Luke's Account of Jesus Before Herod Antipas," *Biblica* 66 (1985) 344-64.

this scene functions within Luke's Passion story.

An important clue to the meaning of the story can be found in 23:8 where Luke mentions that Herod was glad to see Jesus "for he had long desired to see him, because he had heard about him, and he was hoping to see some sign done by him." The reader is taken back to earlier scenes in the Gospel which, in effect, prepare for this Passion incident. The evangelist portrays Herod Antipas (the son of Herod the Great who was living at the time of Jesus' birth, Lk 1:5) as a ruthless, dissolute leader who is intent on destroying Jesus. Herod first enters the Gospel story in 3:1 where his reign is noted as coinciding with the beginning of John the Baptist's ministry ("Herod being tetrarch of Galilee"). Shortly thereafter we hear that Herod imprisons John because the prophet had reproved him for unlawfully taking Herodias as his wife and for "all the evil things (he) had done" (3:18-19). Luke does not narrate the execution of John by Herod but we learn of it in flashback, as Herod's enmity is now beginning to target Jesus (9:7-9). The tetrarch is curious about reports of Jesus' works and that some have identified Jesus with John "raised from the dead." So Herod muses, "'John I beheaded; but who is this about whom I hear such things?' And he sought to see him." Later in the Gospel, Pharisees warn Jesus that Herod now wants to kill him. Jesus lashes back with a direct challenge: "Go and tell that fox, 'Behold, I cast out demons and perform cures today and tomorrow, and the third day I finish my course. Nevertheless I must go on my way today and tomorrow and the day following; for it cannot be that a prophet should perish away from Jerusalem" (13:32-33). Even the desire to "see signs" is a symptom of Herod's character; some of Jesus' enemies had also looked for signs from Jesus "to test him" (11:16).

Now that this strange prophet has been brought to him, Herod's deadly curiosity was on the brink of being satisfied. The scene takes on the air of another hearing. Herod questions Jesus and the Jewish leaders are present, "vehemently accusing him" (23:9). But Jesus does not respond to this murderer of prophets. Luke may wish to portray Jesus here as the suffering servant, who "was oppressed and ... afflicted, yet he opened not his mouth" (Isaiah 53:7).[16] The hearing quickly turns into a scene of mockery as Herod and his soldiers treat Jesus with "contempt."[17] Unlike Mark and Matthew (see Mk 15:17-20; Mt 27:28-31), Luke has no mockery by Roman soldiers at the conclusion of the trial before Pilate. This interlude with Herod and his soldiers serves that purpose.

Finally Herod and his entourage dress Jesus in "gorgeous apparel" and send him back to Pilate. The precise meaning of this investiture is debated. Some contend it is meant to be a royal robe, similar to the mockery by the Roman soldiers in Mark's account (see Mk 15:17-20).[18] For others the term implies a white robe, meant as a mocking sign of Jesus' innocence, or even as a play upon the white robe of candidates for office in Roman society.[19]

But the same description is given for the garb of the heavenly messenger who appears to Peter in Acts 10:30. We can assume, therefore, that Luke considers it a garment of beauty and heavenly dignity. Herod and his court obviously intend it as mockery for this mute and defenseless "prophet" who stands debased before them.[20] As the reader discovers explicitly in the next scene (23:13-16), Herod, too, judges that Jesus is harmless and not guilty of the accusations made against him. In effect two significant witnesses, Pilate and

[16]Luke may take his cue from the Markan scene in which Jesus does not respond to the accusations of the chief priests during the Roman trial; see Mark 15:9.

[17]This same verb is used to introduce the parable of the publican and the sinner; the parable was directed at "those who trusted in themselves that they were righteous and *despised* others (18:9); also in Acts 4:11 which, in referring to the rulers' responsibility for the death of Jesus, cites Psalm 118:22: "This is the stone which was rejected (literally, despised) by you builders, but which has become the head of the corner."

[18]J. Neyrey, *The Passion According to Luke*, 78; F. Matera, *Passion Narratives and Gospel Theologies*, 177-78.

[19]See, for example, R. Karris, *Luke: Artist and Theologian*, 85-87; J. Massyng-baerde Ford, *My Enemy is My Guest*, 127, both of whom believe Luke refers to the white robe of a candidate for office. But if this is Luke's point here it seems extraordinarily subtle.

[20]This generic function of the "gorgeous apparel" seems sufficient rather than trying to decipher a more specific symbolism.

Herod, publicly testify to Jesus' innocence.[21] Once again the multiple levels of Luke's narrative are in play. While Herod and the other characters in the Gospel drama intend this bright vestment as mockery and declare Jesus a harmless innocent, the reader sees it as indicative of Jesus' true dignity and a sign of his God-given power.

The scene closes with a strange footnote. The two rulers who had been enemies "became friends with each other that very day" (23:12). Some interpreters believe this is meant to show that even in death Jesus brings about reconciliation.[22] But it is hard to believe that Luke would consider Herod, whom he casts in such sinister tones, as a model of reconciliation. The real meaning of this sudden alliance is revealed by Peter and John in Acts 4:25-28. After their own release by the Sanhedrin they recall Jesus' sufferings at the hands of the rulers: "for truly in this city there were gathered together against thy holy servant Jesus, whom thou didst anoint, both Herod and Pontius Pilate, with the Gentiles and the peoples of Israel...." The apostles see this unholy alliance as the fulfillment of Psalm 2:1-2, "The kings of the earth set themselves in array, and the rulers were gathered together, against the Lord and against his Anointed." Even though they declare Jesus innocent, these secular powers mock Jesus and ultimately condemn him to death. Their friendship is part of the merging forces of darkness which gather against Jesus.

But Jesus is not broken by interrogation or mockery. To Pilate he gives fearless testimony; to Herod he offers only condemning silence. Once again Jesus' own warning to his disciples comes to mind: "But before all this they will lay their hands on you and persecute you, delivering you up to the synagogues and prisons, and you will be brought before

---

[21]Luke may intend to evoke the law of Deuteronomy 19:15, as may be the case in the two sets of male accusers in the scene of Peter's denial (see, above, 22:54-62); see J. Fitzmyer, *The Gospel According to Luke X-XXIV*, 1480.

[22]See, for example, R. Karris, *Luke: Artist and Theologian*, 85; F. Matera, *Passion Narratives and Gospel Theologies*, 178; J. Fitzmyer, *The Gospel According to Luke X-XXIV*, 1480.

kings and governors for my name's sake. This will be a time for your to bear testimony" (21:12-13). In Luke's narrative, Jesus is faithful to his own teaching.

C) FINAL CONDEMNATION (22:13-25).

His captors haul Jesus from one hearing to another—from the Mount of Olives to the high priest's residence (22:54), from the residence to the council chamber of the Sanhedrin (22:66), from the council chamber to Pilate (23:1), from Pilate to Herod (23:7), and now back to Pilate (23:11). But this would be the final, formal encounter between Jesus and the authorities.[23] Luke skillfully edits the scene to bring to the fore major themes in his portrayal of Jesus as a prophet-martyr: Jesus' innocence from crime, yet his rejection by Israel.[24]

When Jesus is brought back from the session with Herod, Pilate assembles the leaders and "the people" (23:13). Here Luke uses the more significant term, *laos*, emphasizing that it is not just a mob which gathers but all Israel, its leaders and the people.[25] Up to this point in the Passion, the leaders have been the ones who engineer Jesus' arrest and accuse him before Pilate. But now the people themselves seem to abandon their generally favorable view of Jesus and reject him. Luke is not rigid about these categories, however. As

---

[23]J. Neyrey points out that Luke gives attention to the formal elements of a trial in this scene, such as mention of the arrest (23:14a), statement of the charges (23:14b), citing of the interrogation (23:14c), the verdict (23:14d) and supporting verdict by Herod (23:15a), move for acquittal (23:15b), and a judicial warning (23:15c); see, *The Passion According to Luke*, 81.

[24]He is dependent here on Mark 15:6-15, especially for the material in Lk 23:18-25; most of Luke's changes reflect his typical style. For details, see J. Fitzmyer, *The Gospel According to Luke X-XXIV*, 1487-89.

[25]Although Luke can use the terms "crowd" (*ochlos*) and "people" (*laos*) somewhat interchangeably in the Gospel, the latter term has more of a formal collective sense; see J. Neyrey, *The Passion According to Luke*, 110; J. Kodell, "Luke's Use of *Laos,* 'People,' Especially in the Jerusalem Narrative (Lk 19, 28-24, 53)," *Catholic Biblical Quarterly* 31 (1969) 327-43; and J. Crowe, "The *Laos* at the Cross: Luke's Crucifixion Scene," in A. Lacomara (ed.), *The Language of the Cross*, 80-81.

we shall see, a member of the Sanhedrin will come over to Jesus's side (23:50-51), people from Jerusalem mourn his condemnation (23:27), and the multitude will be moved to repentance at the sight of the crucified Jesus (23:48). But at this point in the Passion Luke paints with a broad brush: the prophet sent to Israel meets with rejection by God's people.

Luke intensifies the drama of that fateful choice by the use of two strong contrasts: in the one, the Gentile governor emphatically states Jesus' innocence while the people and leaders demand his crucifixion; in the other, Israel seeks the release of a murderer and insurrectionist, Barabbas, while condemning Jesus who is just and compassionate. Both contrasts are already present in Mark's account, but Luke's presentation sharpens them.

Even Luke admits that Pilate was capable of brutal repression (see 13:1 where we are told that Pilate had mingled the blood of some Galileans with their sacrifices), but in the trial scene he comes through as the only one who speaks on Jesus' behalf. Three times in this scene Pilate affirms that Jesus is innocent: "I did not find this man guilty of any of your charges against him; neither did Herod" (23:14); "nothing deserving death has been done by him" (23:15); "I have found in him no crime deserving death" (23:22). Luke also notes the prefect's repeated desire to release Jesus (23:16, 20, 22). Only because of the mob's relentless demand for crucifixion, does Pilate consent to his condemnation (23:23-25).

Undoubtedly some of Luke's apologetic concerns are at work here; he wants to show that Jesus was not a political revolutionary against the Roman empire. Pilate's declarations of Jesus' innocence and his reluctance to crucify Jesus make that case. The same will be true in the Acts of the Apostles where Roman officials are frequently depicted as favorable to Paul and his companions, despite accusations against them.[26] The contrast between Jesus and Barabbas also serves this purpose. Barabbas *is* a certified revolutionary

[26]See Acts 16:35-40; 18:12-17; 19:28-41; 26:31-32. On this point, see J. Tyson, *The Death of Jesus in Luke-Acts*, 137. On the relationship between Jesus' trial and the trials in Acts, see in particular, J. Neyrey, *The Passion According to Luke*, 89-107.

and murderer; Jesus is not. Luke emphasizes this point (see 23:19, 25). Yet the Jewish leaders and people ironically choose such a man and reject Jesus. Thereby Luke stresses again that Jesus was a victim of injustice, not a guilty criminal.

But as we noted before, there is much more to Luke's message than a concern about Roman opinion of Christianity. Nor should his favorable portrayal of the Roman authorities be overestimated. Luke depicts Pilate as weak and vacillating, as one who was willing to scourge Jesus (23:16, 22), and hand him over to crucifixion even though he had declared Jesus innocent. And Herod is presented as corrupt and as one who mocks and abuses Jesus. These are portrayals hardly calculated to win Roman favor.

The primary importance of this scene for Luke is not the attitude of the Romans but the choice of the Jews.[27] By stripping from the scene such details as the information about the passover custom of releasing a prisoner (Mark 15:6-10) and the efforts of the leaders to stir up the crowd (Mk 15:11), Luke reduces the scene to a stark confrontation between Pilate on one side and the Jewish leaders and people on the other. The Roman wants to release Jesus; the leaders and people want to release Barabbas and condemn Jesus. Luke will end the scene on this note: "Pilate gave sentence that *their demand should be granted*" (23:24); ". . . but Jesus he delivered up *to their choice*" (23:25).

The rejection of Jesus, whom Luke has portrayed as God's unique prophetic messenger to Israel, merges the Passion story with one of the deep currents of the Gospel and Acts, and of the Bible as a whole. The refusal of the Jewish leaders and people to accept Jesus as God's liberator is one more instance of a repeated story in the history of salvation; over and over God's patient love for Israel meets incomprehension and rebuff. Through such rejection the sins of the people were laid bare and they experienced judgment. But just as

---

[27]That "choice" is repeatedly stated by Luke: see 23:18, 23, 24, 25a, 25b; see further on this, J. Neyrey, *The Passion According to Luke*, 82.

emphatically, Luke will acclaim that through the very suffering and rejection Christ experiences, God's forgiveness and salvation would be brought to the whole world (Lk 24:47; Acts 1:8)[28] Through suffering and death the messiah would enter his glory (24:26), and lavish on his disciples the gift of the Spirit (24:44-49).

Even though the condemnation of Jesus is an apparent triumph for the power of darkness, there is a more powerful, and ultimately benign, force at work. As Pilate "hands over" Jesus to crucifixion he paradoxically fulfills the Scriptures and unwittingly moves God's plan of salvation forward to its climax.[29]

VII. The Way of the Cross (23:26-32).

Three elements compose this journey from the court of Pilate to the "Skull Place": Simon carries Jesus' cross (23:26), Jesus warns the daughters of Jerusalem about the the fate of their city (23:27-31), and two criminals are led out with Jesus to their death (23:32).

> [26]And as they led him away, they seized one Simon of Cyrene, who was coming in from the country, and laid on him the cross, to carry it behind Jesus.
>
> [27]And there followed him a great multitude of the people, and of women who bewailed and lamented him. [27]But Jesus turning to them said, "daughters of Jerusalem, do not weep for me, but weep for yourselves and for your children. [29]For behold, the days are coming when they will say, 'Blessed are the barren, and the wombs that never bore, and the breasts that never gave suck!' [30]Then they will begin to say to the mountains, 'Fall on us'; and to the

[28]This way of conceiving salvation history is a major theme of many of the sermons in Acts; see, for example, Acts 2:22-37; 3:12-26; 4:8-12; 10:34-43.

[29]Note the almost technical use of this verb "hand over" (*paradidōmi*) in the Passion narratives. The ultimate agent for Jesus' being "handed over" is God, as the passive tense used in the Passion predictions implies: see 9:44; 18:32.

hills, 'Cover us.' [31]For if they do this when the wood is green, what will happen when it is dry?"

[32]Two others also, who were criminals, were led away to be put to death with him.

A) SIMON CARRIES THE CROSS OF JESUS (23:26).

Jesus' final earthly journey now begins. Having been dragged before so many tribunals—the High Priest, the Sanhedrin, Pilate, Herod—Jesus is now taken to the place of execution. The way of the cross is briefly noted in Mark and Matthew, but Luke develops it, especially by including the encounter between Jesus and the women of Jerusalem.[1]

Luke states that "they" led Jesus away. In the other Gospels, mockery by Roman soldiers had immediately preceded the way to the cross (Mk 15:16-20; Mt 27:27-31; John 19:2-3), so in their cases one can assume that "they" refers to a squad of Roman soldiers. But Luke has no account of mockery by Romans (the mockery by Herod and his soldiers substitutes, see above, 23:11); in fact, no Roman soldier has yet appeared in Luke's Passion story. Therefore, even though it is historically implausible, Luke seems to imply that the ones who lead Jesus out to be crucified are the same Jewish leaders who brought Jesus to trial before Pilate (23:1).

The incident with Simon of Cyrene is already found in Mark's account (Mk 15:21). Luke omits the details about Simon's family background ("the father of Alexander and Rufus," see Mk (15:21) but subtly enriches the symbolism of this moment.[2] The cross is "laid on" Simon and he "carr(ies) it *behind Jesus*" (23:26). The Greek preposition *opisthen* ("behind") and the image of cross-bearing used here link the Simon incident with Jesus' earlier instruction on discipleship:

---

[1]It may be that Luke's predilection for the journey motif is still at work here; see above, Part I, pp. 35-39.

[2]These names may have been familiar to Mark's community; Matthew also omits them (see Mt 26:32); see D. Senior, *The Passion of Jesus in the Gospel of Mark*, 116.

"And he said to all, "If any one would come *after (opis)
me*, let him deny himself and take up his cross daily and
follow me" (9:23).

"Whoever does not bear their own cross and come after
(*opisō*) me, cannot be my disciple" (14:27)

The reader of Luke's Gospel is reminded that the Passion
of Jesus sets the pattern for authentic discipleship.

B) JESUS WARNS THE DAUGHTERS OF JERUSALEM ABOUT THE FATE OF THEIR CITY (23:27-31).

This scene is unique to Luke's Gospel and there is continuing debate about its precise meaning. Some interpret it as
a call to repentance; Jesus deflects the lament of the women
towards themselves and their children, urging them to repent
in the face of coming judgment.[3] But other interpreters consider it to be a pure oracle of doom on Jerusalem and its
inhabitants.[4] A careful reading of the whole scene might
shed some light.

Luke states that Jesus was followed in the way of the cross
by "a great multitude of the people" and "of women who
bewailed and lamented" (23:27. As we have already noted,
Luke sometimes speaks in generalizations about "the crowds"
(*ochloi*) or "the people" (*laos*), just as he does about the
various groups of Jewish leaders. But he can also be quite
specific in reporting the reactions of individuals or segments
of these larger groups. At the trial, the people and the rulers

[3]See, for example, R. Karris, *Luke: Artist and Theologian,* 93-94.

[4]J. Neyrey takes this radical position; see, *The Passion According to Luke,*
108-28. However, he fails to comment on one key aspect of the scene—the fact that
the women bewail and lament *Jesus* (23:27). This makes his contention that the
"Daughters of Jerusalem" symbolize solely "the element of Israel which continu-
ously rejected God's messengers" (p. 110) unpersuasive. Lamenting for Jesus cannot
be construed as an act of rejection. Neyrey is correct that prophetic judgment
against Jerusalem is part of this scene, but Luke also demonstrates in this scene that
not all of the people of Jerusalem reject Jesus—in fact, some lament his condemnation.

seem to be lumped together (see 23:4, 13, 18), but at the cross the "people" (*laos*) stand by "watching," in contrast to the leaders who mock Jesus (see below, 23:35). And "all of the crowd (*ochloi*) who assembled to see" the crucifixion will be struck with remorse after the death of Jesus (23:48).

Therefore we can assume that the crowd that follows Jesus on the way of the cross, unlike those who joined in his condemnation, is not hostile to him. Clearly the women who "bewailed and lamented him" are favorable to Jesus and grieve at his condemnation.[5] Thus Luke shows that Jesus' hold over the people has not been totally broken by the events of the Passion and that some in Israel recognize who he is.[6] Only if this is the case do Jesus' words make sense: "...do not weep *for me*, but weep for yourselves (23:28).... Thus the lament of the women is a counterpoint to the terrible rejection of Jesus by the leaders and people narrated in the previous scene. Through their grief, these Jewish people extend compassion to him.[7]

The words of Jesus to the women (23:28-31) change the mood of the scene. Instead of lamenting Jesus' death, the "daughters of Jerusalem" are warned to lament for themselves and for their children. At times this Passion scene has been entitled, "Jesus consoles the women of Jerusalem." But Jesus' words are not words of consolation but of prophetic judgment against a city that has rejected its messiah.

---

[5]To identify them as "professional mourners" (see J. Fitzmyer, *The Gospel According to Luke X-XXIV*, 1495) and therefore not expressing authentic sentiments of lament for Jesus seems arbitrary; nor does it account for the "great multitude of people" included in the scene.

[6]See, for example 19:48; 21:38, and remarks above, 22:2. Acts will follow through on this. Some Jews will continue their hostility to Jesus by rejecting his apostles and their message; but others, such as the crowds who repent at Pentecost, will be open to the Gospel. This, in fact, keeps continuity with Luke's entire narrative. The infancy narrative presents the Baptist and Jesus originating from a group of devout and faithful Jews.

[7]There may be a possible allusion to Zechariah 12:10, "And I will pour out on the house of David and the inhabitants of Jerusalem a spirit of compassion and supplication, so that, when they look on him whom they have pierced, they shall mourn for him, as one mourns for an only child, and weep bitterly over him, as one weeps over a first-born." This text is explicitly cited in John 19:37.

An important preparation for this scene is found in 19:41-44. After narrating Jesus' triumphant entry into Jerusalem (19:28-40), Luke adds an incident unique to his Gospel. Jesus weeps over Jerusalem and predicts its ultimate destruction as punishment for its refusal to "know the time of (its) visitation" (19:44). The prediction is quite detailed and is an obvious reference to the brutal siege of Jerusalem by the Romans in *A.D.* 70:

> "Would that even today you knew the things that make for peace! But now they are hid from your eyes. For the days shall come upon you, when your enemies will cast up a bank about you and surround you, and hem you in on every side, and dash you to the ground, you and your children within you, and they will not leave one stone upon another in you..." (19:42-44)

Now in the Passion story, Jesus *leaves* Jerusalem and, in addressing the "Daughters of *Jerusalem*," repeats his warning. There are close links in the content of the two oracles of judgment, specifically the reference to "the days are coming" (19:43; 23:29) and the poignant note about the children's fate (19:44; 23:29). The terrible destruction of human life that will take place leads to a tragic beatitude; instead of sterility being a curse, as it always was in the Bible, it now becomes a blessing.[8] Jesus had spoken in the same vein in his final days of teaching in the Temple:

> "But when you see Jerusalem surrounded by armies, then know that its desolation has come near. Then let those who are in Judea flee to the mountains, and let those who are inside the city depart, and let not those who are out in the country enter it; for these are days of vengeance, to fulfill all that is written. *Alas for those who are with child and for those who give suck in those days!* For great distress shall be upon the earth and wrath upon this people..." (21:20-23)

[8]See J. Fitzmyer, *The Gospel According to Luke X-XXIV*, 1496.

Verse 30 alludes to Hosea's words of judgment against an unfaithful Israel:

> "The high places of Aven, the sin of Israel, shall be destroyed. Thorn and thistle shall grow up on their altars; and they shall say to the mountains, Cover us, and to the hills, Fall upon us." (Hosea 10:8).

The city of Jerusalem plays a prominent role in Luke's Gospel.[9] It was both starting point (2:41-51) and endpoint (9:51) for Jesus' mission. But it was also the city that would reject and kill him. The enigma of the Holy City had wrenched a lament from Jesus early in his Galilean ministry:

> "O Jerusalem, Jerusalem, killing the prophets and stoning those who are sent to you! How often would I have gathered your children together as a hen gathers her brood under her wings, and you would not! Behold, your house is forsaken, until you say, 'Blessed is he who comes in the name of the Lord!'" (13:34-35).

Jesus' final words are in the form of a proverb: "For if they do this when the wood is green, what will happen when it is dry?" (23:31).[10] There is an obvious contrast here between the present and the future but the specific meaning is difficult to determine. Who is meant by "they"—the Romans who condemn Jesus and who will destroy Jerusalem? The Jews who have rejected Jesus? Or God who did not spare Jesus and who will surely punish Israel?[11] And what exactly is the

[9] See above, Part I, pp. 36-39.

[10] On the various ways of translating and interpreting this text, see the discussion in J. Fitzmyer, *The Gospel According to Luke X-XXIV*, 1498-99; he suggests four possibilities: 1) "If the Romans so treat me, whom they admit to be innocent, how will they treat those who revolt against them?"; 2) "If Jews so treat me who have come to save them, how will they be treated for destroying me?"; 3) "If human beings so behave before their cup of wickedness is full, what will they do when it overflows?"; 4) "If God has not spared Jesus, how much more will Judaism, if impenitent, learn the seriousness of divine judgment?"

[11] On use of impersonal "they" for God, see Luke's parable of the rich man and his barns which concludes, "This night *they* will require your soul of you" (12:20).

"green" and the "dry" wood? A comparison between the time of Jesus and a future time when Jerusalem would be destroyed? Or between Jesus who is just and Israel who is guilty?

Proverbs are often difficult to decipher and this one is no exception. Given the context, where the women lament Jesus' impending death and he warns about the future destruction of Jerusalem, it seems best to understand the proverb along these lines: If I who am just suffer death at the hands of the Romans, what can those who are guilty expect?

In any case the overall meaning of Jesus' words to the women is clear: they form a prophetic warning of God's judgment against the city of Jerusalem because of its infidelity in rejecting Jesus. As Luke writes his Gospel, of course, the terrible Jewish war of *A.D.* 66-70, with its near total destruction of Jerusalem and its temple, had already taken place. Luke, in retrospect, interprets this historical tragedy as divine punishment for the sins of Israel.[12] Modern readers of the Gospel may find this a jarring portrayal of Jesus; it certainly clashes with interpretations of the Gospel which screen out all elements of judgment in favor of Jesus' compassion and mercy. Although Luke surely puts mercy at the very center of his portrayal of Jesus, he does not consider it incompatible with a strong dose of judgment. Choosing evil rather than good has real consequences and the note of judgment in the Gospel acknowledges this truth.[13]

One final question remains about this troubling episode in the Passion. In telling the women to "weep" does the Lukan Jesus hold out to them the possibility of repentance? Or does this oracle leave no hope for a doomed and guilty people?[14]

[12]Both Mark and Matthew have similar interpretations of the destruction of Jerusalem; see, D. Senior, *The Passion of Jesus in the Gospel of Mark*, 24-28; *The Passion of Jesus in the Gospel of Matthew*, 177-81.

[13]On the theme of judgment in Luke-Acts, see J. Neyrey, *The Passion of Jesus in the Gospel of Luke*, 124-28.

[14]Recent interpreters are also divided over this issue: R. Karris, for example, concludes: "It seems abundantly clear that in 23:27-31 Luke is emphasizing repentance." (*Luke: Artist and Theologian*, 93). However, after a detailed analysis, J.

Looking only at Jesus' words to the women, one could conclude that there is no invitation to repentance here. The
"weeping" Jesus speaks of are not tears of repentance like
Peter's (22:62) but tears of lament and grief over tragedy.
But when this incident is put in the wider context of the
Passion narrative and Luke's Gospel, the implication of repentance cannot be excluded. Luke always holds out that
possibility, as we shall see in the example of the repentant
criminal (23:39-42) and the crowds who are stricken with
remorse at Jesus' death (23:48). And in Acts those who listen
to Peter's sermon are moved to repentance because of it
(Acts 2:37—42). The great crowd includes people of Judea
and "all who dwell in Jerusalem" (2:14).

Both judgment and the challenge to repent can coexist in
the Gospel, including Jesus' prophetic warning to the daughters of Jerusalem. In Luke's view, those caught up in the
tragedy of Jerusalem's siege experienced God's wrath, but
the invitation to repent and experience God's mercy remained
in force. Jerusalem's "house," its glorious temple, would be
forsaken, but with God there was always an "until"—until
God's people would say, "Blessed is he who comes in the
name of the Lord" (13:35).[15]

C) THE TWO CRIMINALS (23:32).

Along with Simon and the crowd, there are two others
who form the strange retinue of the Messiah. Only Luke
notes the presence of the two criminals accompanying Jesus
on the way to the cross (23:32).[16] This prepares for the scene

---

Neyrey states: "The address of Jesus [i.e., 23:27-31] is not a call to repentance at
all..." (*The Passion According to Luke*, 121).

[15]On this see R. Tannehill, "Israel in Luke-Acts: A Tragic Story," *Journal of
Biblical Literature* 104 (1985) 69-85. Referring to Lk 13:35, he concludes that Luke
sees a "lingering hope" for Israel, but the note of tragedy still dominates the
evangelist's view of Israel.

[16]In contrast to Mark and Matthew who use the term *leistai* ("thieves" or "bandits"), Luke refers to them by the more generic term *kakourgoi* ("criminals", "evil-
doers").

at the cross (23:39-43) and is further confirmation of Jesus' statement at the passover meal: "For I tell you that this scripture must be fulfilled in me, 'And he was reckoned with transgressors'; for what is written about me has its fulfillment." (22:37). All during his life Jesus had a special bond with the sinner and outcast, earning his enemies' contemptuous label, "a glutton and a drunkard, a friend of tax collectors and sinners" (7:34). Now Jesus would walk to death with these same companions.

VIII. Crucifixion and Death (23:33-49).

The climax of the Passion story is now at hand. As Jesus' strange entourage of Simon Cyrene, the lamenting crowds, and two condemned criminals arrive at the Skull Place, Luke presents a series of vivid episodes: the crucifixion (23:33-34), the mockery (23:35-38), the repentant criminal (23:39-43) and, finally, the death of Jesus and its profound impact on the bystanders (23:44-49).

> [33]And when they came to the place which is called The Skull, there they crucified him, and the criminals, one on the right and one on the left. [34]And Jesus said, "Father, forgive them; for they know not what they do." And they cast lots to divide his garments.
>
> [35]And the people stood by, watching; but the rulers scoffed at him, saying: "He saved others; let him save himself, if he is the Christ of God, his Chosen One!"
>
> [36]The soldiers also mocked him, coming up and offering him vinegar, [37]and saying, "If you are the King of the Jews, save yourself!" [38]There was also an inscription over him, "This is the King of the Jews."
>
> [39]One of the criminals who were hanged railed at him, saying, "Are you not the Christ? Save yourself and us!" [40]But the other rebuked him, saying, "Do you not fear God, since you are under the same sentence of condemnation? [41]And we indeed justly; for we are receiving the due reward of our deeds; but this man has done nothing

wrong." [42]And he said, "Jesus, remember me when you come into your kingdom." [43]And he said to him, "Truly I say to you, today you will be with me in Paradise."

[44]It was now about the sixth hour, and there was darkness over the whole land until the ninth hour, [45]while the sun's light failed; and the curtain of the temple was torn in two. [46]Then Jesus, crying with a loud voice, said "Father, into thy hands I commit my spirit!" And having said this he breathed his last. [47]Now when the centurion saw what had taken place, he praised God, and said, "Certainly this man was innocent!" [48]And all the multitudes who assembled to see the sight, when they saw what had taken place, returned home beating their breasts. [49]And all his acquaintances and the women who had followed him from Galilee stood at a distance and saw these things.

A) CRUCIFIXION AT THE PLACE CALLED "SKULL" (23:33-34).

As in other parts of the Passion story, Luke's account is leaner than that of Mark. A number of details are dropped or altered, while some new elements are introduced. The overall effect is the enhancement of Luke's characteristic themes.

The execution place is called "skull"; Luke omits the Aramaic term "Golgotha" found in the other Gospels (see Mk 15:22 and parallels). There is no mention of the offer of wine mixed with myrrh ("gall," in Matthew's version) as in Mk 15:23. Luke's description of the hideous moment of the crucifixion itself is stark and understated: ". . . there they crucified him and the criminals, one on the right and one on the left" (23:33).

A new element is the addition of Jesus' words of forgiveness for those responsible for his death: "Father, forgive them; for they know not what they do" (23:34). These words are not found in a number of important ancient manuscripts, leading to the suspicion that they were added later. However, this reading was known to the early fathers and it fits Luke's characteristic language and theology.[1] The emphasis on forgiveness is typical of this Gospel, especially from a Jesus who teaches his disciples to love their enemies.[2] And the attributing of his enemies' actions to "ignorance" echoes similar texts in Acts (see, for example, 3:17; 13:27; 17:30). Casting it in the form of a prayer to his Father also fits Luke's manner of presentation, complementing Jesus' prayer on the Mount of Olives (22:42) and at the moment of death (23:46). A strong parallel to Jesus' prayer for forgiveness are Stephen's words directed to the Risen Christ as he is about to die. "Lord, do not hold this sin against them" (Acts 7:60). The meshing of this verse with Luke's theology and the parallels in Acts are not decisive arguments for the originality of this verse in the Passion story, but do make it strongly probable. It may have been omitted from some early manuscripts when anti-Jewish feeling among Gentile Christians made such forgiveness on Jesus' part seem too lavish.[3]

Those crucified were usually stripped, and the Gospels assume that Jesus also suffered this humiliation.[4] The casting of lots for Jesus' garments (23:34b) is not simply a bit of information; it is a citation of Psalm 22:18, ". . . they divide

[1] See the discussion in J. Fitzmyer, *The Gospel According to Luke X-XXIV*, 1503 and I. Howard Marshall, *Commentary on Luke*, 867-68, both of whom conclude on internal evidence that the saying is genuine, while conceding that the textual evidence precludes certainty on this point.

[2] On the love of enemies tradition in Luke, see above, p. 81, n. 58. Forgiveness of sins (or Luke's specific vocabulary of " release" [aphesis] from sins—see 4:18) is a major theme of Luke's Gospel. Salvation is experienced as liberation from sin and, therefore, "release" from sin is proclaimed at the inauguration of Jesus' mission (4:18), carried out in his acts of healing (e.g., 5:17-26) and given as a commission to the post-Easter community (24:47). On this motif, see R. Tannehill, *The Narrative Unity of Luke-Acts*, 103-109.

[3] Assuming that Luke was written after the destruction of Jerusalem and that this tragedy was interpreted as punishment for the rejection of Jesus (see above, p. 125). Jesus' prayer for forgiveness for those who condemned him may have appeared problematical to some recipients of the Gospel. See the comments of I. Howard Marshall, *Commentary on Luke*, 867-8.

[4] On the process and meaning of crucifixion, see M. Hengel, *Crucifixion* (Philadelphia: Fortress, 1977), esp., 22-32; J. Fitzmyer, "Crucifixion in Ancient Palestine, Qumran Literature, and the New Testament," *Catholic Biblical Quarterly* 40 (1978), 493-513.

my garments among them, and for my raiment they cast lots." Allusion to this great lament Psalm of the Old Testament was already present in Mark's version of the Passion (Mk 15:24) and will be fully exploited by Matthew.[5] The Psalm expresses the anguished prayer of the just Israelite who, even as suffering and death seem about to overwhelm him, puts complete confidence in God. God will vindicate the trust of the just one who suffers. Luke's presentation of Jesus in his Passion, as one who suffers rejection and mockery yet never loses trust in God, is in full harmony with this fundamental theology.[6]

B) MOCKERY (23:35-38).

Jesus now becomes the victim of mockery as he hangs on the cross. This cruel scene also has links to Psalm 22 and to the wisdom tradition of the suffering just one. In Psalm 22:6-7 the just one cries out, "But I am a worm, and no man; scorned by men, and despised by the people. All who see me mock at me, they make mouths at me, they wag their head".... The device of mockery is played out more extensively in the book of Wisdom, where the enemies of the just Israelite scorn his trust in God (see, for example, Wisdom 2:10-20).

Luke shapes this scene to fit his own perspective. Since he had eliminated the temple issue from the trial, he also omits it here.[7] Also in Luke's account the "people" (*laos*) significantly do not join in the mockery; they "stood by, watching" (23:35). This is a change from the versions of Mark and Matthew who have the "passersby" join in the taunting of Jesus (see Mk 15:29; Mt 27:39). As we have already noted,

---

[5]On Psalm 22 and its place in Mark and Matthew, see D. Senior, *The Passion in the Gospel of Mark*, 118, 123-24; *The Passion in the Gospel of Matthew*, 127-30, 136-42.

[6]The presence of this motif in Luke's Passion account is emphasized by R. Karris, *Luke: Artist and Theologian*, esp., 95-98.

[7]Compare Mk 15:29, "Aha! You who would destroy the temple and build it in three days..."; on the trial scene, see above, pp. 99-105.

Luke presents at least a portion of the people as responsive to Jesus.[8] Some of them follow him in the way of the cross and grieve at his condemnation (23:27), and presumably the same multitude will be driven to repentance by his death (23:48).

In this scene Luke has two sets of mockers hurl their challenges at Jesus, the rulers and the soldiers. The scene is punctuated with another sort of mockery, the placing of a placard on the cross. The words of mockery help accentuate the issues at stake in Jesus' death: his identity as Messiah, his ability to save others, and, foundational to everything, his relationship with God.

The first mockery comes from the "rulers." In contrast to the "people", the rulers scoff at Jesus and taunt: "He saved others; let him save himself, if he is the Christ of God, his chosen One!" (23:35). Luke injects into their words important theological motifs that have characterized his entire portrait of Jesus. The verb to "save" (*sōzein*) sums up Jesus' mission of salvation that is a fundamental theme of Luke's theology, a theme announced by the angels at Jesus' birth (2:11) and by Jesus himself in the synagogue of Nazareth (4:18-19), and a reality carried out in his powerful ministry of healing and teaching.[9]

In their mockery, however, the rulers twist a profound truth about salvation. Jesus has "saved others" but he cannot "save himself." Salvation comes from God and God would deliver Jesus from death through resurrection. This will be a major theme of the Acts of the Apostles.[10] But Jesus' own ministry would be characterized in pouring out his life to save others. Thus Jesus had taught that the physician cannot "heal himself" (4:23), and if someone tried to "save" their

---

[8]See above pp. 121-22.

[9]See above, Part I, pp. 21-28.

[10]In Acts Luke proclaims the "reversal" of Jesus' fate by God. The Jesus condemned by human beings is "saved" by God through resurrection, thereby becoming the agent of salvation for the world (e.g., Acts 2:22-24, 31-33; 3:14-15, 26; 4:10-12; 5:30-31; 10:39-43; 13:30-39). On this motif, see J. Neyrey, *The Passion According to Luke*, 133-46.

own life, they would instead "lose it." Only if they "lost" their life for Jesus' sake would they save it (9:24).

Their taunt brings to the surface another powerful current of the Gospel: "If he is the Christ of God, his Chosen One!" The conditional wording, "if he is . . . ", triggers for the reader memories of the Sanhedrin's question, "if you are the Christ . . . (22:67), and more haunting still, Satan's testing of Jesus in the desert: "If you are the Son of God (4:3, 9). . . . The withering assault of evil upon Jesus now comes to its full intensity.

This entire scene is drenched in irony. The rulers are confident that this helpless and condemned opponent is anything but a savior or the Christ or God's chosen one. But the reader of Luke's drama knows the truth. Jesus *is* the "Christ of God," as divine messengers had announced at his birth (2:11) and Peter had acclaimed earlier in the Gospel (9:20). And Jesus was God's "chosen one" as the voice from heaven had thundered at the transfiguration (9:35).

The next in this procession of torment are the soldiers (23:36). As noted above, Luke does not mention a mockery by Roman troops at the conclusion of the trial before Pilate (contrast Mk 15:16-20); the abuse of Herod and his soldiers seems to substitute for this. But the scene at the cross shows that Luke is not out to exonerate the Romans. Soldiers, too, mock Jesus. Mark places this incident in the very last moment before Jesus' death (see Mk 15:36), but Luke inserts it here, clearly indicating that he considers it a mockery of Jesus.

The soldiers offer him vinegar or sour wine to drink, a detail that once more triggers remembrance of a great Old Testament lament psalm: "They gave me poison for food, and for my thirst they gave me vinegar to drink" (Psalm 69:22). Similar to the report about casting lots for Jesus' garments, which cites Psalm 22, this tortuous detail helps portray Jesus as the suffering just one, whose only support is with God.[11] The soldier's words echo the charges of the

---

[11]Note that Luke omits any reference to Elijah's coming; compare Mk 15:36.

Roman trial scene: "If you are the King of the Jews, save yourself!" The term "king of the Jews" smacks of the political accusations raised there (see above, 23:1-5). The soldiers, too, speak in terms that evoke haunting memories of Satan's test in the desert ("If you are...") and their sneering, "save yourself" continues to bring the theme of salvation to the fore.

Unlike Mark and Matthew who refer to the inscription on the cross prior to the mockery of Jesus (see Mk 15:26), Luke notes it here, in the midst of the mockeries (23:38, note the explicit link: "There was *also* an inscription....") Even Luke's literal wording suggests that the inscription itself is meant to be an insult: "The King of the Jews, this man!" By branding Jesus as a foolish pretender to political kingship, the inscription on the cross insures that the injustice of the trial and the ridicule heaped on Jesus by Herod follow him to his death. But once again, the reader knows the deeper truth: Jesus *is* a king but not in the manner his opponents expect. Instead of being a sign of ridicule as intended, the inscription on the cross becomes a bold proclamation of Jesus' royal dignity.

The mockery, therefore, shows the unbridgeable gap between Jesus and his enemies. They still deride his supposed messianic identity and his claim to be close to God. He is ridiculed for his royal pretensions. But the reader knows the paradoxical truth of the Gospel: through his Passion Jesus performs the final, decisive act of his mission of salvation. Through suffering, the Christ, the anointed king, fulfills God's plan of salvation and enters into glory (see 24:26, 44-47). Through death, Jesus would complete his "exodus" (9:31) and be exalted at the right hand of God.

C) THE TWO CRIMINALS (23:39-43).

This brief scene, found only in Luke's Gospel, is a brilliant example of the evangelist's literary technique and theological perspective.[12] Mark's Passion story had noted without com-

---

[12]Some commentators consider this the highpoint of Luke's crucifixion scene

ment that "those who were crucifed with (Jesus) also reviled him" (Mk 15:32). But Luke develops this passing reference into a miniature drama all its own. The two criminals who had accompanied Jesus on the way of the cross and had been crucified on each side of him, now exemplify radically different responses to Jesus.

There is a close connection to the previous scene (23:35-38). Two sets of mockers had hurled their insults at Jesus; now two more characters encounter the crucified Jesus. Luke, in fact, favors pairs and contrasting examples.[13]

Luke's hand is particularly evident in the content of this scene.[14] The words of the unrepentant criminal continue the challenge to Jesus' identity as Messiah and savior, the issue that dominated the mockery scene (23:35-38). Even one of those condemned with Jesus is not touched by his passion and taunts him: "Are you not the Christ? Save yourself and us!" (23:39).

But the second criminal has a very different spirit. His response is a model of repentance. First of all, he "silences" or "rebukes" (*epitimōn*) his fellow criminal, exemplifying Jesus' own instruction in the Gospel to "rebuke (*epitimēson*) your brother if he sins" (17:3). He reminds his companion in death, "Do you not fear God, since you are under the same

(see, for example, J. Fitzmyer, *The Gospel According to Luke X-XXIV*, 1508; E. Earle Ellis, The Gospel of Luke [New Century Bible; Grand Rapids: Eerdmans, 1981, 267]. But this may overstate the case; the death of Jesus and the reactions to it (23:44-49) remain the natural climax of the scene.

[13]On Luke's tendency to present people in pairs, see J. Navone, *Themes of St. Luke* (Rome: Gregorian University Press, 1970), 224-29. Luke also typically presents contrasting examples: for example, Mary and Martha (10:38-42), the elder brother and the prodigal son (15:11-32), the rich man and Lazarus (16:19-31), the publican and the sinner (18:9-14), etc.; see, further, J. Neyrey, *The Passion According to Luke*, 134.

[14]Commentators debate whether Luke is drawing on a previously existing source here; see for example, J. Fitzmyer, who concludes that the scene is "inspired by Mark 15:32c" ("And those crucifed with him kept taunting him."), but is "probably derived from 'L'" (The Gospel According to Luke X—XXIV, 1507). I. Howard Marshall admits that the episode "is manifestly written in Luke's own style" but "betrays sufficient Palestinian features to suggest that Luke was not creating out of nothing" (*Commentary on Luke*, 871). The extraordinary amount of Lukan motifs present here argues in favor of its being a composition of the evangelist.

sentence of condemnation?" Failure to "fear God" is a sign of blind arrogance, similar to the "unrighteous" judge in Jesus' parable (who "neither feared God nor regarded people," 18:2,4). By contrast, Mary's magnificat acclaims that mercy is lavished on those who "fear God" (1:50). The repentant criminal openly confesses his sin: "And we indeed (are punished) justly; for we are receiving the due reward of our deeds..." (23:41), and, most important of all, he turns to Jesus for help (23:42), calling on the name that is a source of salvation for all the world (see Acts 4:12). Thus the repentant criminal recognizes something that all of the mockers have missed: this crucifed man is, in fact, the Christ, the savior of the world. As a result of his repentance, the criminal is promised a place in "paradise" with Jesus that very day (23:43). The criminal's trust in Jesus and his willingness to repent have brought him salvation. The entire process of conversion is exemplifed in this mini-drama.

But more is at stake here than a paradigm of repentance. Equally important is the profound christology implicit in this scene. First of all, the repentant criminal offers further testimony to Jesus' innocence: "this man has done nothing wrong." His testimony refutes that of the mockers, just as the decisive statement of the centurion will do at the moment of Jesus' death (23:47). Despite the attempts of his enemies to portray Jesus as unjust, the truth breaks through. Jesus is God's just one who suffers unjustly yet does not swerve from his God-given course.

Secondly, the fate of the repentant criminal illustrates the saving power of Jesus' death. Some interpreters of Luke have questioned whether the evangelist attributes any salvific consequences to the death of Jesus as such. Salvation came through the gift of the Spirit, following on the resurrection of Jesus.[15] Few interpreters would want to deny that in Luke's view the resurrection, the ascension, and the sending of the

---

[15]The influential study of H. Conzelmann is a prime example of this point of view: "...there is no trace of any Passion mysticism (in Luke's Passion narrative), nor is any direct soteriological significance drawn from Jesus' suffering or death. There is no suggestion of a connection with the forgiveness of sins." See, *The Theology of Saint Luke* (London: Faber and Faber, 1960), 201.

Spirit on the community are seen as God's vindication of Jesus and as the full expression of his saving power. But the suggestion that Luke attributes no saving significance to Jesus' death itself has been rightly challenged in some recent studies.[16] Luke does not present the saving consequences of Jesus' death in the same manner as Paul or other New Testament authors do, but this scene of the Passion story demonstrates that Luke did attribute saving power to the death of Jesus.

The whole thrust of the scene is that Jesus is savior through his death. The word "to save" (*sōzein*) is repeated throughout the crucifixion scene (23:35 [2x], 37, 39). Implicitly, the repentant criminal puts his faith in the crucified Jesus, just as a whole stream of broken people had done throughout the Gospel.[17] The experience of healing or forgiveness was an experience of God's definitive salvation, promised for the end time but anticipated now in the renewal of their bodies and spirit. Thus the recurring phrase in the Gospel: "your faith has saved you." The repentant criminal asks that Jesus remember him when he comes "into your kingdom" (23:42). The sense is that of a future moment: "when". . . . But Jesus' response emphasizes the immediacy of salvation: "Truly, I say to you, *today*, you will be with me in Paradise." By his obedient death, Jesus completes his journey and returns to his Father; through suffering the Christ "enters into his glory" (24:26). Through his faith in Jesus, the repentant criminal shares in that experience of salvation; for him, entrance into

[16]See, for example, J. Fitzmyer, *The Gospel According to Luke I-IX*, 219-27; A. George, "Le sens de la mort de Jésus pour Luc," *Revue Biblique* 80 (1973), 186-217; R. Glöeckner, *Die Verkündigung des Heils beim Evangelisten Lukas* (Mainz: Grüenwald, 1976); J. Kodell, "Luke's Theology of the Death of Jesus," in D. Durken (ed.), *Sin, Salvation, and the Spirit* (Collegeville: Liturgical Press, 1979), 221-30; R. Fuller, "Luke and the *Theologia Crucis*," in D. Durken (ed.), *Sin, Salvation, and the Spirit*, 214-220; R. Zehnle, "The Salvific Character of Jesus' Death in Lucan Soteriology," *Theological Studies* 30 (1969) 420-44. The soteriology of Luke is a major thesis of both R. Karris, *Luke: Artist and Theologian*, passim, and J. Neyrey, *The Passion According to Luke*, esp., 156-92.

[17]See J. Neyrey, *The Passion According to Luke*, 135, who notes Luke's emphasis on those who plea with Jesus for healing or forgiveness: see Lk 4:38-39; 5:12-13; 7:3-4, 8-9; 8:41-50; 9:38; 18:37-42.

the kingdom happens immediately.[18]

This sense of immediacy is also typical of Luke's theology. The angel announces to the shepherds, "...for to you is born *this day* in the city of David a Savior, who is Christ the Lord" (2:11). In the Nazareth synagogue, Jesus tells the congregation that Isaiah's announcement of future salvation for the poor and oppressed is fulfilled "*today*" in their hearing (4:21). When Jesus forgives the paralytic his sins and enables him to stand up and walk, the crowd is amazed and gives glory to God because they "have seen strange things *today*" (5:26). When Jesus comes to dine in Zacchaeus' house it is a visit that brings salvation: "*Today* salvation has come to this house" (19:9). . . .

In concert with all of the New Testament, Luke views the fullness of salvation as a future event at the end of human history (e.g., 21:25-27). But through the powerful word and the healing touch of Jesus salvation has already begun to break into the world.[19] His death for others was the summit of Jesus' ministry, his ultimate act of healing. The words and actions of Jesus at the passover meal had already proclaimed that his body was given for others, his blood poured out as a new covenant.[20] It is not surprising, therefore, that evidence of salvation should explode into view in the Passion. The healing of the severed ear of the high priest's slave (22:51), reconciliation with Peter (22:61-62), forgiveness extended to his executioners (23:34), and the impulse of the crowds to repent at the cross (23:48) are other symptoms of salvation breaking through within the Passion story. The repentant criminal's bold prayer draws from Jesus the most staggering

---

[18]In Matthew (27:51-53) the impact of Jesus' death breaks open the tombs and liberates those trapped in death. For Matthew, too, the death of Jesus has immediate saving consequnces. On this text, see D. Senior, *The Passion in the Gospel of Matthew*, 143-47.

[19]This experience of salvation connected with the ministry of Jesus continues in the post-Easter mission of the church; on Luke's theology of salvation and his eschatology, see F. Danker, *Luke*, 86-90; J. Fitzmyer, *The Gospel According to Luke I-IX*, 231-35; R. Maddox, *The Purpose of Luke-Acts*, 100-57; R. O'Toole, *The Unity of Luke's Theology*, 33-61, 97-159.

[20]See above, pp. 59-64.

promise of all: this day the condemned criminal would accompany Jesus to paradise.[21]

Finally, we should note that this scene presents the experience of salvation in tones typical of Luke. Jesus is once more associated with a malefactor, as he had predicted at the last supper (22:37) and just as he had done throughout his ministry.[22] The Son of man who had come "to seek and to save the lost" (19:10) would restlessly seek those on the margins until his last breath was drawn. "Release for captives" (4:18) was his first promise and his last act.

And the promise that a repentant criminal would taste the joys of "paradise" is also a characteristic Lukan way of conceiving salvation. "Paradise" in the Bible evokes images of exotic bliss, of unending joy and celebration.[23] Building on the paradise image of a banquet, Jesus had promised that the powerless and therefore the uninvited would head the guest list in the Kingdom of God: "the poor and maimed and blind and lame" (14:15-24). To the great offense of his opponents, Jesus had befriended public sinners, earning the title "a friend of tax collectors and sinners" (7:34). Luke presents Jesus as dying in the same provocative manner, promising a repentant criminal that he would share paradise with God's son that very day.

D) THE DEATH OF JESUS (23:44-49).

The climax of the Passion story comes with the death of Jesus. Luke paints this scene with sharp, quick strokes. The fateful moment is signaled by two cosmic signs, the sun's

---

[21]J. Neyrey points out that the criminal also follows Jesus' instruction on bold prayer: "Ask, and it will be given you; seek, and you will find; knock, and it will be opened to you. For everyone who asks receives, and he who seeks finds, and to him who knocks it will be opened" (11:9-10); see *The Passion According to Luke*, 135.

[22]See above, 22:37 and Part I, pp. 24-28.

[23]The story of the lush primeval garden in Genesis 2 is the starting point for all biblical reflection on paradise; see J. Jeremias, "*paradeisos*," in G. Kittel (ed.), *Theological Dictionary of the New Testament*, Vol. V, 765-73. R. Karris considers the word "paradise" the "key to an analysis of 23:43" because it provides a link to Luke's motif of food and banquet; see, *Luke: Artist and Theologian*, 102-103.

light fails and the veil of the temple is torn in two (23:44-45). Jesus dies with a prayer to his Father on his lips (23:46), while the witnesses—a centurion, the crowds, friends, and faithful women disciples—are overwhelmed by the power of his death (23:47-49). The evangelist does not report Jesus' cry of dereliction from Psalm 22, nor the bystanders' statement that he is calling on Elijah—both elements of Mark and Matthew's narratives (see Mk 15:34-36; Mt 27:46-49). The powerful scene that results eloquently sums up Luke's theology of the death of Jesus.

The Darkness

As the decisive moment of the Passion approaches, darkness spreads over the earth (23:44). This dramatic sign was already present in Mark's account (Mk 15:33); Luke adds the explanatory detail, "while the sun's light failed" (23:45). This confirms that it is not a local phenomenon, but a cosmic sign affecting the whole world. A threatening darkness was one of the events the Bible associated with the end of the world. In the prophet Joel, the Lord warns:

"And I will give portents in the heavens and on the earth, blood and fire and columns of smoke. The sun shall be turned to darkness, and the moon to blood, before the great and terrible day of the Lord comes" (Joel 2:30-31).

Amos, another prophet of judgment, has a similar text: "'And on that day,' says the Lord God, 'I will make the sun go down at noon, and darken the earth in broad daylight" (Amos 8:9).

The Tearing of the Temple Veil

The tearing of the temple veil is a more ambiguous symbol. In Mark and Matthew's versions, the tearing of the veil *follows* the death of Jesus and seems to be an effect of it (see Mk 15:38; Mt 27:51).[24] But in Luke the tearing of the veil

---

[24]There are subtle differences between Mark and Matthew, however. For Mark

precedes the moment of death and is fused on to the cosmic sign of darkness, suggesting that it may have a different meaning than it does for Mark or Matthew. For some interpreters, however, the tearing of the veil in Luke's account is still to be seen as a consequence of Jesus' redemptive death. It may signal the opening of the wall that sin placed between God and humanity, similar to the more explicit statement of this theme in the letter to the Hebrews (9:6-28). Or it signals the breaking down of the barrier of hostility that separates Jew from Gentile, a symbol used in the letter to the Ephesians (2:14).[25] For others the tearing of the veil represents an implicit judgment against the temple, with Jesus himself now the new temple, a theme clearly present in Mark and John.[26]

But these interpretations may be influenced too much by the meaning of this sign in the accounts of Mark and Matthew. Recent studies have tried to view this temple sign on strictly Lukan terms. For some this implies a more benign significance to the tearing of the veil. They point out that the temple seems to fare much more positively in Luke than it does in the other Gospels.[27] By having the tearing of the veil precede the death of Jesus rather than being a consequence of it, Luke may be attempting to soften the negative meaning of this sign. The tearing of the veil might be also connected

---

the tearing of the veil is primarily a sign of judgment against the temple; for Matthew the tearing of the veil is the first of a series of signs (opening of the earth, splitting of rocks, opening of tombs) that ultimately free those trapped in death. The element of judgment against the temple is moderated in Matthew's account, in favor of the liberating action of opening the tombs. On these interpretations, see D. Senior, *The Passion of Jesus in the Gospel of Mark*, 126-29; *The Passion of Jesus in the Gospel of Matthew*, 142-43.

[25]See, J. Fitzmyer, *The Gospel According to Luke X-XXIV*, 1514.

[26]R. Karris, for example, believes that a text such as Acts 22:17-21, where Paul recounts his experience of hearing the voice of the Risen Christ in the temple, suggests that Luke thinks of Jesus himself as the new temple; see, *Luke: Artist and Theologian*, 106-107.

[27]See above, [131, n.]; also, F.D. Weinert, "The Meaning of the Temple in Luke-Acts," *Biblical Theology Bulletin* 11 (1981) 85-89; "Luke, the Temple, and Jesus' Saying about Jerusalem's Abandoned House (Luke 13:34-35)," *Catholic Biblical Quarterly* 44 (1982) 68-76; and, on Acts, "Luke, Stephen and the Temple in Luke-Acts," *Biblical Theology Bulletin* 17 (1987) 88-91.

with the prayer of Jesus that follows.[28] In this interpretation
the tearing of the veil is a moment of revelation, prompting
Jesus' acclamation. Jesus, in effect, has a vision of God
through the now separated curtain that had shrouded the
inner sanctuary. That encounter with God triggers Jesus'
final prayer in which he entrusts his life into the hands of the
Father—similar to the vision that precedes Stephen's death
in Acts 7:55.

But if it is Luke's intention to suggest that Jesus sees God
through the torn veil of the Temple, the evangelist is extraordinarily subtle.[29] The "tearing of the veil" is on its face
level an act of violence to the temple. The veil is not "opened"
(as would seem to be appropriate for a vision of God) but
"torn down the middle." Therefore it makes sense to relate
this sign to the darkening of the sun; both are ominous signs.
By linking the tearing of the temple veil to the darkness,
Luke implies that these two events have a similar function
and meaning. They set the stage for what follows. In the
ancient world forboding cosmic signs were often reported at
moments of historic significance.[30] But the biblical texts from
Joel and Amos confirm that in the biblical drama darkness

[28]This is the interpretation of D. Sylva, "The Temple Curtain and Jesus' Death in
the Gospel of Luke," *Journal of Biblical Literature* 105 (1986) 239-50. He observes
that in the Greek, the phrase, "but the veil of the temple was torn in two" (23:45)
can be read as a lead into Jesus' prayer in the next verse, just as easily as connecting
it with the preceding sign of the sun's light failing.

[29]Although there are parallels between Stephen's and Jesus' death (see above,
23:34), this particular connection seems forced. In Acts, Luke leaves no doubt that
Stephen sees a vision: "But he, full of the Holy Spirit, gazed into heaven and saw
the glory of God, and Jesus standing at the right hand of God; and he said, 'Behold,
I see the heavens opened, and the Son of man standing at the right hand of God.'"
(Acts 7:55-56). This vision confirms the exaltation of Jesus and serves as a dramatic
validation for the entire speech of Stephen. But there is no real indication in the text
that Jesus saw a vision of God through the torn veil of the temple. The circum-
stantial evidence of worship which Sylva appeals to—the "ninth hour" as the hour
of prayer, the acclamation of praise by the Centurion, the witnesses "beating their
breasts"—does not add up to a "temple" scene at the crucifixion.

[30]Josephus reports the words of Mark Antony to the high priest and ruler
Hyrcanus, how "the very sun turned away" from looking on the foul deeds of those
who rebelled against Caesar (see Josephus, *Antiquities* 14.12, 3); the Roman his-
torian Lucan in his *Civil War* reports that at the battle of Pharsalus, the sorrow of
the gods caused them to eclipse the sun; see C.H. Talbert, *Reading Luke*, 224-25.

over the earth has more than generic meaning. It is a sign of
the chaos and doom that accompanies the end of the world.
It is part of God's judgment against a sinful age. The tearing
of the sacred veil shrouding the Holy of Holies, through
which only the High priest could enter on the Day of Atonement, was a warning that the impending destruction and
judgment of the final days would engulf even the house of
God.

This mood of judgment meshes with Luke's theology.
While Luke reverences the Jerusalem Temple and has the
Jerusalem church continue to worship there, he has also
reported Jesus' prophetic warnings that Jerusalem and its
temple would suffer terrible destruction as part of God's
judgment.[31] The guardians of the temple, the chief priests,
would be the prime agents in his death. And in Acts these
same leaders would expel the apostles from the temple (e.g.,
Acts 4:1-3; 5:17-18). The temple was God's house and thus
was a place of prayer. But it was also a place controlled by
those who rejected Jesus and the Gospel and would therefore
not escape God's purifying judgment.

In fact during his final days of teaching in the temple,
Jesus had given warning about both the temple's destruction
and threatening signs within nature: "As for these things [the
beautiful stones and votive offerings of the temple] which
you see, the days will come when there shall not be left here
one stone upon another that will not be thrown down" (21:6).
And the final day of the Lord would include "signs in sun
and moon and stars..." (21:25). Even on his way to crucifixion Jesus had warned the "daughters of Jerusalem" about
those days of mourning and destruction (23:28-31).

That mood of threat and darkness is evoked here as the
Passion comes to its decisive moment. When his captors
were about to seize him, Jesus had said, "This is your hour,
and the power of darkness" (22:53). Now that hour comes,
with its full demonic fury tearing at the life of God's son.

[31]See above, 23:26-31, and the balanced treatment by J. Tyson, *The Death of
Jesus in Luke-Acts*, esp. 107-10.

These signs of catastrophic destruction—the quenching of the sun's light and destruction even within the house of God— measure the terrible test Jesus must endure.

Jesus' Final Prayer

Jesus' last words are a prayer shouted into the dark heaven: "Father, into thy hands I commit my spirit" (23:46). The words are taken from Psalm 31, one of the Bible's most eloquent prayers that swings in mood from anguish to thanksgiving.[32] The line used in Luke's text comes from the opening section of the Psalm and expresses fundamental trust in God's fidelity:

> "In thee, O Lord, do I seek refuge; let me never be put to shame; in thy righteousness deliver me!
> Incline thy ear to me, rescue me speedily!
> Be thou a rock of refuge for me, a strong fortress to save me!
> Yea, thou art my rock and my fortress; for thy name's sake lead me and guide me, take me out of the net which is hidden for me, for thou art my refuge.
> Into thy hand I commit my spirit; thou hast redeemed me, O Lord, faithful God." (Psalm 31:1-6)

The only significant change the evangelist has made in citing the Psalm is the addition of the address "Father." This ancient prayer of trust is now molded into the language of the Lukan Jesus.[33] Three times in Luke's Passion story Jesus had addressed his Father in prayer, entrusting his life to God's will on the Mount of Olives (22:42), pleading for forgiveness on behalf of his enemies (23:34) and now, at the

---

[32] See the comments of C. Stuhlmueller, *Psalms 1* (Old Testament Message 21; Wilmington: Michael Glazier, 1983) 178-83.

[33] On the role of prayer in Luke, see A.A. Trites, "The Prayer Motif in Luke-Acts," in C.H. Talbert (ed.), *Perspectives on Luke-Acts* (Special Studies Series 5; Danville, VA: Association of Baptist Professors of Religion, 1978) 168-86; D. Senior, "Jesus in Crisis: The Passion Prayers of Luke's Gospel," in C. Osiek & D. Senior, (eds.), *Scripture and Prayer* (Wilmington: Michael Glazier, 1988)

moment of death. Earlier in the Gospel, Jesus had exulted in the Spirit and praised his "Father" for entrusting "all things" to him (10:21). And when the disciples asked how to pray, Jesus' model prayer had begun, "Father, hallowed be thy name .." (11:2). When Jesus had come of age he declared to his startled parents: "Did you not know that I must be in my Father's house?" (2:49). Now at the end of his mission Jesus would cross the threshold of death and dwell forever at his Father's right hand.

Luke clearly states that this spirit of trust in a faithful God accompanies Jesus in death: "*And having said this*, he expired" (23:46b). The contrast with the account of Mark is revealing.[34] Jesus' last words in Mark are taken from the lament psalm 22: "My God, my God, why hast thou forsaken me?" (Mk 15:34). The spirit of this great prayer is also one of trust but the words cited stress the anguish of one who searches for God's elusive presence in the midst of suffering and darkness. In Mark's account Jesus does not die praying the psalm. Only after Jesus' anguished cry is interpreted as an appeal to Elijah and after a sponge full of vinegar is offered to him, does the moment of death come with a wordless scream (Mk 15:37). Mark's theology emphasizes the stark reality of Jesus' death for others.

By omitting this material and fusing Jesus' prayer of trust onto the instant of death, Luke has created a different mood. Even though the powers of darkness seem triumphant, Jesus dies confidently, entrusting his spirit into the hands of his Father. The power of darkness has been defeated by Jesus' trust in a faithful God. Thus Luke brings to term the christology he has portrayed from the beginning of the Gospel. The Jesus who was fully committed to God's will and had set his face toward Jerusalem, stayed the course. He had followed the way set out for the Son of Man.[35] Now his "exodus" was

[34]On Jesus' final prayer in Mark, see D. Senior, *The Passion of Jesus in the Gospel of Mark*, 123-26. Matthew's account also uses Psalm 22 but moves somewhat in the direction of Luke by having Jesus repeat the psalm ("Jesus cried again" Mt 27:50) at the instant of death; see D. Senior, *The Passion of Jesus in the Gospel of Matthew*, 139-41.

[35]J. Fitzmyer sees a hint of this in the repetition of the word "hand over" (*para-*

completed and he would return to God in order to lavish on the world the Spirit of forgiveness and salvation.

In so depicting Jesus' death, Luke created a model of a heroic Christian death. The fierce attacks of injustice fall short; they cannot discredit or break Jesus. Even in the agony of death, Jesus witnesses to God's life-giving and sustaining power. Thereby Jesus the martyr-prophet dies in a way that would inspire countless generations of witnesses to follow. Luke himself tells the first of these martyrdom stories in the account of Stephen's death in Acts. As he is executed, Stephen prays: "Lord Jesus, receive my spirit" (Acts 7:59).

The Witnesses

Three sets of witnesses react to the death of Jesus, each in a fashion distinct to Luke's theology. The centurion, presumably the officer of the Roman soldiers who had crucified Jesus and had joined in mocking him (23:36), has a profound change of heart: "Now when the centurion saw what had taken place, he praised God, and said, "Certainly, this man was just" (23:47). The language strongly reflects Luke's theology. In contrast to Mark and Matthew where the centurion confirms Jesus' identity as Son of God (Mk 15:39; Mt 27:54), in Luke the key issue is Jesus' character as a "just" man. The Greek word used here, *dikaios*, can also be translated (as in the Revised Standard Version) as "innocent." Some interpreters prefer to stress this aspect of the word; thereby the Roman officer, along with Pilate and Herod earlier in the Passion, becomes another witness to Jesus' innocence of the political charges that had been brought forward at the trial.[36] Jesus dies as an innocent victim of injustice, similar to the martyrs of Judaism.[37]

---

didōmi) in the Passion narrative; the Jesus who had been handed over so many times to his enemies (9:44; 18:32; 20:19; 22:53; 24:7) now hands his own life over to God; see, *The Gospel According to Luke X-XXIV*, 1514.

[36]See, for example, J. Massyngbaerde Ford, *My Enemy is My Guest*, 134-35; she cites G.D. Kilpatrick, "A Theme of the Lucan Passion Story and Luke 23:47," *Journal of Theological Studies* 43 (1942) 34-36.

[37]Some interpreters would contend that Jewish martyrdom stories such as those

While this motif is present, the word *dikaios* understood as "just" suggests that deeper and richer biblical currents are also at work here. Jesus is "just" because his entire life and mission was one of faith in God. He proves his "justice" in remaining true to God's will even when tested by the terrible power of evil and faced with the jaws of death.[38] For Luke Jesus embodies the "just" man, that prototype of the faithful Israelite portrayed in the book of Wisdom: "Those who trust in God will understand truth, and the faithful will abide with God in love, because grace and mercy are upon God's elect, and God watches over the holy ones" (Wisdom 3:9).

The centurion who was present at Jesus' death "sees" through these events the profound truth about Jesus and is moved to "praise God." Both elements fit Luke's perspective. From the first moments of his ministry Jesus' life has a strong public character; what he says and does fulfills the promise of Scripture and gives witness to God's saving power.[39] That public witness does not cease with the Passion. As a prisoner Jesus gives bold testimony to his interrogators (22:67-71), pronounces a prophetic oracle to the Jerusalem crowds (23:28-31), forgives his executioners (23:34), promises a repentant criminal a share in paradise (23:43), and dies with a public prayer of trust in God (23:46). All of this has a powerful revelatory character which breaks through the hos-

---

found in the Martyrdom of Isaiah and II and IV Maccabees have had a strong influence on Luke's Passion narrative as a whole. M. Dibelius was one of the first to propose this and his opinion has been influential; see *From Tradition to Gospel* (New York: Scribners, n.d.) 201-02. However, more recent studies have contested this. While Luke certainly portrays Jesus as a martyr-prophet, martyrdom is not the only or dominant pattern for the Passion story. See the discussion in B. Beck, "'Imitatio Christi' and the Lucan Passion Narrative," in W. Horbury and B. McNeil (eds.), *Suffering and Martyrdom in the New Testament* (Cambridge: Cambridge University Press, 1981), 28-47; F. Georg Untergassmair, *Kreuzweg und Kreuzigung Jesu: Ein Beitrag zur lukanischen Redaktionsgeschichte und zur Frage nach der lukanischen "Kreuzestheologie"* (Paderborner Theologische Studien 10; Paderborn: Schöningh, 1980) 156-71; R. Karris, "Luke 23:47 and the Lucan View of Jesus Death," *Journal of Biblical Literature* 105 (1986) 65-74.

[38]R. Karris, *ibid.*, and F. Matera, "The Death of Jesus According to Luke: A Question of Sources," *Catholic Biblical Quarterly* 47 (1985) 469-85, esp., 483-84.

[39]This is strongly laid out in the Nazareth synagogue scene; see, above, Part I, 18-21.

tility of a Roman soldier and draws from him a prayer of praise to God and public testimony to Jesus. Such outbursts of praise to God line the Gospel of Luke, from the shepherds of Bethlehem (2:20) to the blind man of Jericho (18:43). "Praise" is the faith response to a recognition of God's saving presence.[40] The centurion recognizes God's saving presence in the events of the Passion, and particularly in the heroic death of the just Jesus.[41]

It is significant that the centurion gives public testimony to what he sees in Jesus. This element of witness is a major theme of Luke's theology.[42] In his final appearance to his disciples, the Risen Christ will command them to be "witnesses of these things" (24:48)—that is, "that the Christ should suffer and on the third day rise from the dead, and that repentance and forgiveness of sins should be preached in his name to all nations, beginning at Jerusalem" (24:46-47). The centurion is the first one in the Gospel to give witness to the meaning of Jesus' suffering, the beginning of a stream of public testimony that will continue with the women who discover the empty tomb (24:1-12) and become a torrent in the post-Pentecost preaching of the community in Acts.

The "entire assembled crowds" (23:48) also "see" the things that have taken place and, they, too react in a significant way. They return home "beating their breasts." This is an element unique to Luke; none of the other evangelists report the reaction of the crowds after the death of Jesus. As we had noted before, Luke portrays the crowd in a subtle fash-

[40]R. Karris notes that in Luke, "praising God" is a way of responding to a revelation of God's saving power: e.g., 2:20; 5:25, 26; 7:16; 13:13; 17:15; 18:43; Acts 4:21; 11:18; 21:20. See *Luke: Artist and Theologian*, 110; also R. O'Toole, *The Unity of Luke's Theology*, 225-60.

[41]Luke's reference to seeing "what had taken place" (23:47) refers most immediately to the death of Jesus but probably extends to all of the events which the centurion had witnessed on Golgotha: Jesus' forgiveness of his enemies, his promise to the repentant thief, the cosmic portents of the darkness and the tearing of the veil, his final prayer and his death.

[42]See, A.A. Trites, *The New Testament Concept of Witness* (SNTSMS 31; Cambridge: Cambridge University, 1977) 128-53, 175-98; J. Navone, *Themes of St. Luke*, 199-209; R.J. Dillon, "Easter Revelation and Mission Program in Luke 24:46-48," in D. Durken (ed.), *Sin, Salvation, and the Spirit*, 254-56.

ion; while some of them at least demand the death of Jesus (23:18), there are also indications of continuing sympathy and remorse (see 23:27). The witness of Jesus' faithful death seems to pierce through their consciousness and they, too, repent of their sin of rejecting the Messiah. The gesture of "beating their breasts" recalls that of the tax collector hovering far from the temple altar, "beating his breast, saying, 'God, be merciful to me a sinner'" (18:13).[43]

A final group of witnesses are also mentioned: "all those who knew him" and "the women who had followed him from Galilee" stand at a distance from the cross and "saw these things" (23:49). The presence of women at the cross is noted by all the evangelists (see, Mk 15:40; Mt 27:55; John 19:25). Only Luke refers to "those who knew him." Some interpreters see an allusion to Psalm 38:11 here, "My friends and companions stand aloof from my plague, and my kinsmen stand afar off."[44] However, the connotation of the psalm is negative; the aloofness of the psalmist's friends compounds his sufferings. But a different mood seems at work in Luke's text. By describing the women as those who "had followed him from Galilee" Luke implies they continue to be faithful to Jesus. These same women will witness the burial of Jesus (23:55-56) and will become the first to proclaim the resurrection (23:1-12). Their "seeing" of the events of Jesus' death, therefore, bears fruit in their resurrection faith.

The same seems to be implied for the "acquaintances" of Jesus (literally, "those who knew him"). Luke is probably referring to the disciples of Jesus. As noted above, Luke softens the Markan image of the disciples within the Passion story.[45] While they do display weakness—vividly played out in the case of Peter—Jesus' prayer at the passover meal has

---

[43]Sylva's contention that this is a gesture associated with temple worship because the publican is in the temple in Lk 18:13 (the only other occurrence of the gesture in Luke) seems strained; he offers no intrinsic reason why beating the breast would be an appropriate gesture in the temple; see, D. Sylva, "The Temple Curtain and Jesus' Death in Gospel of Luke," 247.

[44]See, I. Howard Marshall, *Commentary on Luke*, 877; F. Danker, *Jesus and the New Age*, 242.

[45]See above, 71-75.

insured that they would "remain with me in my trials" (22:28). Therefore Luke does not mention the disciples' flight at the moment of the arrest (compare Mk 14:50-51) and has Jesus' glance draw Peter back from the brink of apostasy (22:61). At the same time, Luke did not completely refurbish the image of the disciples presented in the Markan tradition. Their weakness was evident at the supper dispute over greatness (22:24-27), in their misunderstanding of Jesus' instructions (22:38, 49-50), in their fearful sleep before the moment of the arrest (22:45), and, of course, in Peter's denials (22:54-62). Luke's light touch in describing the disciples' somewhat distant and passive presence at the death of Jesus fits this mixed image. They have stayed with Jesus through the "test" of his suffering and death, but barely.[46] Their weak faith will be in evidence again when they refuse to believe the testimony of the women (24:11), in the discouragement of the Emmaus disciples (24:13-25), and in the fright and doubts of all the disciples when they encounter the Risen Christ (24:36-41). Only with the coming of the Spirit would the full force of the disciples' faith be ignited.

Even if subtly stated, Luke already demonstrates the saving power of Jesus' death. His unconditional act of trust in God defuses the powers of darkness and gives such eloquent witness to God's fidelity and mercy that it begins to transform those able to see it.

IX. The Burial (23:50-56).

The Passion story ends quietly with the account of Jesus' burial in a newly cut rock tomb.

[46]"This (i.e., the weakened faith of the apostles) is indicated even in 23:49, for Jesus' acquaintances stand 'at a distance.' This indicates a weakened discipleship that is unwilling to pay the price of discipleship. They are like Peter, who followed Jesus 'at a distance' (22:54) but denied him when his own life was threatened. Nevertheless, it is important that they are present at the crucifixion 'to see these things' for from this group of disciples will come Jesus' witnesses to the people. They must experience these events not only because they are key events for understanding Jesus and his mission about which the witnesses must later speak, but also because they have direct relevance for the future experience of the witnesses themselves." R. Tannehill, *The Narrative Unity of Luke-Acts*, 272.

[50]Now there was a man named Joseph from the Jewish town of Arimathea. He was a member of the council, a good and righteous man, [51]who had not consented to their purpose and deed, and he was looking for the kingdom of God. [52]This man went to Pilate and asked for the body of Jesus. [53]Then he took it down and wrapped it in a linen shroud, and laid him in a rock-hewn tomb, where no one had ever yet been laid. [54]It was the day of Preparation, and the sabbath was beginning. [55]The women who had come with him from Galilee followed, and saw the tomb, and how his body was laid; [56]then they returned, and prepared spices and ointments. On the sabbath they rested according to the commandment.

There is a muted yet expectant atmosphere to this scene. Two sets of characters come forward as the dead body of Jesus is removed from the cross and taken for burial. Luke skillfully reworks Mark's version of this scene to underscore once again characteristic themes of his Gospel.

The figure of Joseph is more evidence of Luke's nuanced characterization of the opponents of Jesus. Just as some parts of the crowd would not remain hostile to Jesus (see 23:48), so too some of the group most resolutely opposed to him prove open to conversion. Similar examples can be found in Acts with the measured judgment of the Pharisee Gamaliel (Acts 5:33-39) and the report that "many of the priests were obedient to the faith" (Acts 6:7).

Joseph's origin is "from the Jewish town of Arimathea" (23:50). By explicitly stating a "*Jewish* town" (compare Mk 15:43, "Joseph of Arimathea") Luke may be calling attention to Joseph's Judean origin—a point balanced by the *Galilean* women who are also present at the burial (23:55).[1] Thus the entire span of Jesus' ministry from Galilee to Judea is evoked here, fitting homage for one crucified as "King of the Jews" (23:38).

---

[1]The term "Jewish" in this verse almost certainly refers to Judea, as distinct from Galilee or Samaria; see J. Fitzmyer, *The Gospel According to Luke X-XXIV*, 1526.

Mark's narrative had already identified Joseph as "a respected member of the council who was also himself looking for the kingdom of God" (Mk 15:43). Luke builds on this startling fact in adding that Joseph was "a good and righteous man who had not consented to their purpose and deed" (23:50-51). The key word *dikaios*, "just" or "righteous," was already applied to Jesus himself (see above, 23:47). Joseph is "just" because he refused to accede to the false judgment of the Sanhedrin.[2] Like the centurion, Joseph is able to recognize in Jesus an innocent, godly man. Luke does not yet describe Joseph as a disciple but he is on his way to becoming one. He is "looking for the kingdom of God" like those examples of sturdy Jewish piety, Simeon and Anna, in the infancy narrative (see 2:25, 38). His innate goodness separates him from the rest of the council and leads him to the courageous act of claiming the body of one who was condemned by the Sanhedrin and executed by the Romans.

In so describing Joseph, Luke not only provides another vignette of courageous witness but also reasserts the innocence of Jesus. The Romans and Herod and now a member of the Sanhedrin itself proclaims that Jesus is not a criminal but a just man tragically rejected. At the same time Luke backhands Jesus' opponents. Joseph had not consented to their "purpose" or their "deed"—both of which were heinous in Luke's view.

Luke describes the burial in crisp yet reverent terms.[3] Joseph requests and is granted the body of Jesus, wraps it in a linen shroud, and places it in a "rock-hewn tomb, where no one had ever yet been laid" (23:53). The detail about a new tomb (which Luke has in common with John 19:41) may suggest a royal burial. The royal Messiah Jesus had ridden into his city of Jerusalem on a colt "on which no one has ever yet sat" (19:3). As befitting his dignity, the crucified

[2]One must assume that the "council" referred to here is the same as that which gathered to condemn Jesus (22:66) even though different Greek terms are used in each case.

[3]Omitted are details concerning Pilate's question whether Jesus was already dead and the confirmation of that fact from the centurion; see Mk 15:44-45.

body of the "king of the Jews" is laid in a tomb untouched by death.

Luke notes the time: it was the "day of Preparation, and the sabbath was beginning" (23:54; see Mk 15:42). Throughout the Gospel and Acts the evangelist shows great respect for the Jewish law and that is the case here. Burial, even for a crucified person, was to be before sundown. Deuteronomy (21:22-23) prescribed that the body of an executed person was not "to remain all night upon the tree" but was to be buried "the same day." In the New Testament period this text was applied to crucifixion.[4] Concern for the law closes this scene, too; the women rest on the Sabbath "according to the commandment" (23:56). Luke continues to make his case: Jesus and his followers are "just."

The Passion story ends with the women (23:55). The ones who had followed Jesus on his liberating mission in Galilee (8:1-3) and come up with him to Judea, and who had stayed with him through the test of the Passion (23:49), are the last to leave the stage. They "see" the tomb and the fact that his body was placed within it. Then they leave—but only to prepare for their return (23:56). They gather spices and ointments, fitting accompaniment for Jesus' royal burial. But their return to the tomb can come only after the Sabbath rest because of respect for the law (23:56).

Luke's exquisite irony is apparent. These faithful disciples, who do not give up on Jesus and who return to minister to him, will be the first witnesses of the resurrection. The tenacious faith of the women in Luke's story is in sharp contrast to the weak response of the other disciples.

From Suffering to Glory: The End of Luke's Gospel.

Luke's story about Jesus does not end with the Passion narrative. The one crucified as "King of the Jews" and buried

---

[4]A connection between Deut 21:22-23 and crucifixion is found in Qumran literature; see "Crucifixion in Palestine, Qumran, and the New Testament," in J. Fitzmyer, *To Advance the Gospel* (New York: Crossroad, 1981) 134-40.

reverently in a newly cut rock tomb bursts from the bonds of death, igniting the faith of his followers, giving them a world-wide mission, and, finally, returning in triumph to his Father. Even then the story does not end, but spills over into Acts, as the Risen Christ sends upon the Jerusalem community the gift of God's Spirit, enabling the apostles to take up their liberating mission in Jesus' name.

Although the Passion narrative is our focus, we need to briefly trace how Luke follows through on his description of the suffering and death of Jesus.

Each evangelist proclaims the resurrection in a distinctive fashion.[1] As did Matthew, Luke absorbs the account of the discovery of the empty tomb from Mark's Gospel (Mk 16:1-8; comp. Mt 28:1-8; Luke 24:1-2) but goes far beyond his source, adding several appearances of the Risen Christ to his followers and a final departure.

THE RESURRECTION DAY.

Luke narrates four major episodes. All of them take place on Sunday and all of them happen in and around Jerusalem.

a) The Empty Tomb.

The first event of this triumphant day is the discovery of the empty tomb (24:1-12). Luke draws this story from Mark but adds his characteristic touches. The dawn arrival of the women at the tomb bringing spices for the anointing of Jesus' body (24:1) links this story with the conclusion of the Passion narrative (24:55-56). Instead of a sealed tomb they discover the entrance stone rolled away and an empty burial chamber. Two men "in dazzling apparel"—obviously hea-venly messengers—appear to the perplexed women and drive

---

[1]On the resurrection accounts see, R. Fuller, *The Formation of the Resurrection Narratives* (Philadelphia: Fortress, 1980); H. Hendrickx, *Resurrection Narratives* (London: Geoffrey Chapman, 1984); J.F. Jansen, *The Resurrection of Jesus Christ in New Testament Theology* (Philadelphia: Westminster, 1980); P. Perkins, *Resurrection* (New York: Doubleday, 1984).

home the basic message: "Why do you seek the living among the dead? Remember how he told you, while he was still in Galilee, that the Son of man must be delivered into the hands of sinful men, and be crucified, and on the third day rise." (24:5-7). The empty tomb and the messengers' words are the first proclamation of the easter event. They also take the reader back over the Gospel story. Jesus who had proclaimed God's salvation from Galilee to Jerusalem, and who had suffered the test of the Passion, has triumphed over death.

The women (identified for the first time as Mary Magdalene, Joanna, Mary the mother of James, and "the other women," 24:10) "remember" Jesus' words and return from the burial place to proclaim the easter message to the "the eleven and all the rest." But the apostles' solidarity with Jesus is still weak; they do not accept the women's testimony.[2] Peter himself comes to the tomb, peers at the burial cloths (see 23:53), but is puzzled by what he sees (24:12).[3] His "seeing" is not yet the penetrating understanding of revelation that transformed the centurion or the women themselves. Until the Risen Christ breaks through

[2]See above, comments on crucifixion scene (23:49). Luke reaffirms this view in 24:22-23.

[3]This verse is omitted by some ancient manuscripts and many modern commentaries and translations have questioned its authenticity. However, it is well attested in important major manuscripts and was well known among the early fathers; see J. Fitzmyer, *The Gospel According to Luke X-XXIV*, 1542; F. Neirynck, "Le récit du tombeau vide dans l'évangile de luc (Lc 24, 1-12)," in *Miscellanea J. Vergote. Orientalia Lovaniensia Periodica* 6-7 (1975-76), 427-41 (reprinted in *Evangelica.* Collected Essays by Frans Neirynck [F. Van Segbroeck, ed.; Leuven: Peeters, 1982], 297-312, and "Lc. xxiv 12 Les temoins du texte occidental" *Novum Testamentum* supplement 47 (1978) 45-60 (reprinted in *Evangelica*, 313-28). Some consider it a tradition Luke had in common with John (see John 20:3-10). However, it is not impossible that Luke himself added this element to the story. It may be prompted by the reference to a special appearance to Peter already found in Mark (16:7) and well attested in tradition (see 1 Cor 15:5). Luke himself will refer to this appearance in the report of 24:34. In addition Luke's subsequent narrative *needs* this kind of action; in 24:24 the Emmaus disciples observe that "some of those who were with us went to the tomb, and found it just as the women had said; but him they did not see." For further redactional arguments in favor of Lukan composition, see F. Neirynck, "The Uncorrected Historic Present in Lk. XXIV.12," *Ephemerides Theologicae Lovanienses* 48 (1972) 548-553 (reprinted in *Evangelica*, 329-34); J.M. Ross, "The Genuineness of Luke 24:12," *Expository Times* 98 (1987) 107-08.

the dullness of Peter and the other apostles they are unable to believe fully the stupendous reality of the resurrection (see below, 24:34, 41, 52-53).

b) On the Way to Emmaus.

The account of Jesus' encounter with two disciples on the road to Emmaus and their meal together is an exquisite narrative unique to Luke. Only the extended ending of Mark's Gospel (16:12-13) has echoes of a similar story. The scene is crammed with Lukan motifs. The two disciples are on a journey, but one that seems to reverse the purposeful journey of Jesus himself. Their hopes stripped away by the death of Jesus, they leave Jerusalem, the city they had entered in triumph with Jesus only a few days before. The events of the Passion had brought not illumination but despair. They still treasured the memory of Jesus, "a prophet mighty in deed and word before God and all the people" (24:19), but they could not understand how his suffering and death had any meaning for the redemption of Israel (24:21). Even the women's testimony about the empty tomb and a "vision of angels" declaring his resurrection, could not reinflate their hope.

The Risen Jesus joins them on the road. Luke deftly notes that they were unable to recognize him, a sign of Jesus' glorified state. After listening to their review of woe, Jesus interprets all of the Scriptures and shows their harmony with his own destiny (24:25-27).[4] Luke's Jesus had inaugurated his mission in the synagogue of Nazareth by declaring that what he said and did would fulfill God's word (4:21). That same motif dominates the end of the Gospel. Everything about Jesus, especially his passage from suffering to glory,

---

[4]The attempt to pinpoint specific passages intended by Luke seems fruitless. The evangelist, in harmony with all of the New Testament, interprets the Hebrew Scriptures as a whole from a christological perspective. "The whole Christian story—the story of Jesus and of the church—is the fulfillment of the whole purpose of God as set forth in the whole of the Old Testament," R. Maddox, *The Purpose of Luke-Acts*, 142.

drew its source and meaning from God's will expressed in the Scriptures.

Not only does Jesus interpret the Scriptures, he also breaks bread with his hope-weary disciples. The interlude at table is one of Luke's masterstrokes. Throughout the Gospel Jesus had shared meals with those who hungered for his word: the disciples, the tax collectors and sinners, Zacchaeus, the Galilean crowds. The meal image, too, emerged time and again in his teaching. On the eve of Passover, with death on his mind, he had dined with his disciples one final time and pledged that he would eat with them again in the Kingdom of God (22:14-30).

With death's grip snapped, the Risen Christ again blesses the bread, breaks it and gives it to his disciples (24:30; see 9:16; 22:19). That gesture, so typical of Luke's Jesus, opens their eyes. In the breaking and giving of bread—the revealing sign of Jesus' whole mission of giving himself for the salvation of the world—the two disciples finally see and understand. That same inclusive and nourishing symbol of a meal shared would be cited again in Acts; Peter would remember that the Risen Christ manifested himself "...to us who were chosen by God as witnesses, who ate and drank with him after he rose from the dead" (Acts 10:41)[5]

There is little doubt that by this powerful blend of the word interpreted and the bread broken and shared, the evangelist evokes for his community the meaning of the Eucharist.[6] In celebrating that sacred meal, the church would remember Jesus' own meals with outcasts and sinners. They would remember, too, his final passover meal where serving at table expressed the meaning of Jesus' life and death for others. Enacting that meal in memory of him would make them witnesses of the gospel.

---

[5]An alternate reading in Acts 1:4 may also refer to these post-Easter meals: "And while eating with them he charged them not to depart from Jerusalem".... In other readings the word "staying" replaces "eating."

[6]On the overall theme of meals in Luke and their eucharistic connotations, see R. Karris, *Luke: Artist and Theologian*, 47-78; R. O'Toole, *The Unity of Luke's Theology*, 46-47; C.H. Talbert, *Reading Luke*, 229-31; E. LaVerdiere, *Luke*, 287-88.

Their hope restored, the two disciples turn back to Jerusalem with a mission. Their disillusionment has evaporated; now they can retrace Jesus' own purposeful journey to the Holy City. They, too, now exemplify the perseverance under trial demanded of the followers of Jesus, the prophet-martyr. They proclaim the resurrection to the other disciples, only to learn that the Risen Jesus has already appeared to Simon.

c) Appearance to the Jerusalem Community.

Luke now adds a final, climactic encounter between the Risen Christ and the assembled group of disciples (24:36-49). The incident is special to Luke but has some similarities to John 20:19-23. As the Emmaus disciples report their experience on the road to the Jerusalem community, the Risen Jesus is suddenly present again.[7] The disciples are dazzled and frightened, supposing that they are seeing a "spirit" (24:36). Jesus' words to them confirm that their faith in his triumph over death has not yet taken hold: "Why are you troubled, and why do questionings arise in your hearts?" (24:38). To disprove that he is a mere ghost and to affirm that it is really the same crucified Jesus who is now raised in glory, the story emphasizes the "physical" aspects of the Risen Jesus. The disciples are to observe his hands and feet (recalling the crucifixion wounds?), to "handle" him in order to see that he has "flesh and bones" (24:39). Joy—a sign of incipient faith in the Risen Christ—begins to dawn, as Jesus asks for something to eat to confirm it is really him and he is truly alive (24:41-43). That characteristic sign of a meal shared is once again the validating trademark of Luke's Jesus.

The most important part of this scene is the commission Jesus now gives to his disciples (24:44-49). These verses are a distillation of Luke's theology.[8] As he had done on the road to Emmaus, Jesus proclaims that all of the Scriptures find

---

[7]By details such as this sudden, mysterious appearance, Luke subtly communicates the glorified state of the Risen Christ.

[8]On this, see R. Dillon, *From Eye Witnesses to Ministers of the Word*, and his article, "Easter Revelation and Mission Program in Luke 24:46-48," in D. Durken, *Sin, Salvation, and the Spirit*, 240-70.

their fulfillment in him. All of the hopes for salvation, all of the warnings about judgment and purification, all of the promises of forgiveness, all of the yearning to be a whole people at peace—all of this finds its expression in Jesus and his mission. His interpretation "opened their mind to understand the scriptures"—just as his words brought wisdom burning in the hearts of the disciples on the road.

The summation of that message of fulfillment is now restated by Jesus: "Thus it is written. . . " (24:46). The heart of the message is Jesus' own death and resurrection—"the Christ should suffer and on the third day rise from the dead." From that center flows all the rest: repentance and forgiveness of sins are to be preached in Jesus' name to all nations, beginning with Jerusalem; the disciples themselves are to be the "witnesses" of these things; and the force and dynamism of this mission will come from the Spirit, the "promise of my Father" which the Risen Christ would send to his church. In condensed form, Luke has summed up the entire Gospel and laid out the program for the Acts of the Apostles. Repentance and forgiveness were the heartbeat of Jesus' mission, proclaimed in his words, enacted in his healing touch and provocative outreach to sinners. Empowered by the Spirit, the apostles and the other early missionaries would take that same message to the ends of the earth.

d) Ascension

Luke's Gospel ends with a mixture of finality and expectancy. The Risen Jesus leads his disciples out of Jerusalem to Bethany, the same village from which his triumphant procession into the city had been staged (19:28). For Jesus, journeying is now complete. In fulfillment of God's word, he had set his face for Jerusalem (9:51), had endured suffering and death, and had faithfully entrusted his spirit to God (23:46). His "exodus" (9:31) from death to life had been consummated. Now he would ascend to his Father, to be immersed in that love bond which had fueled his mission (10:21-22).

But for the disciples, the end is only the beginning. Jesus' last act is to bless these witnesses who would carry the gospel from Jerusalem to the ends of the earth (24:50-51). They return to Jerusalem "with great joy" and to its temple where they "continually [were] blessing God" (24:53).

The final words of Luke's narrative loop the reader's attention back to the beginning of the Gospel. While Zechariah had been performing his routine duties as priest in the temple, an "Angel of the Lord" had shattered his calm with startling news of unexpected life (1:8). The infant Jesus, too, had been brought to the temple to hear Simeon's haunting words of prophecy: this child was the embodiment of God's salvation, "a light for revelation to the Gentiles and for glory to thy people Israel" (2:32). In that temple, Jesus himself, fresh with manhood, would declare that "he must be in his Father's house" (2:49). And near the end of his life-long journey, he would come again to take possession of the house of God, purifying it, warning its errant caretakers of God's coming judgment, teaching the people within its porticoes (19:45-21:38).

From that temple and its city, the Spirit-filled community of disciples would ultimately turn to the world (Acts 1:8). Thus the Gospel ends on an unfinished, expectant note. Acts picks up the narrative, recalling the events after the death of Jesus up to the Ascension,[9] and beginning to trace the gradually widening circle of the community as it moved from Judea, to Samaria, and beyond the confines of Israel. What happens geographically and culturally, is paralleled by a radi-

---

[9]There are some irreconcilable differences between the Gospel and Acts concerning the Ascension. In the Gospel it occurs on Sunday, the same day on which the empty tomb was discovered and Jesus appeared to the various groups of disciples (see 24:50-51). In Acts there is an interval of forty days between the Passion and the ascension (Acts 1:1-11). The specific purpose of each narrative may explain the discrepancy; in the Gospel an immediate ascension serves Luke's purpose of linking the glorification of Jesus closely to his death and resurrection. The ascent is the final phase of Jesus' return to God. In Acts Luke is more concerned with the transition from the age of Jesus to the age of the church; in this context the Risen Christ's instruction of his apostles helps recapitulate the gospel story and prepare for the coming of the Spirit. On the meaning of the ascension in Luke's theology, see J. Fitzmyer, "The Ascension of Christ and Pentecost," *Theological Studies* 45 (1984) 409-40; on the textual problems connected with Acts 2:1 and Lk 24:51, see M. Parson, "The Text of Acts 1:2 Reconsidered," *Catholic Biblical Quarterly* 50 (1988) 58-71.

ating stream of witnesses, moving from Peter, John and the Jerusalem church, to Paul, the "chosen instrument" (Acts 9:15) who would take the gospel beyond the horizons of Israel.[10]

Thus the final chapter of Luke's Gospel provides an important transition between the life of Jesus and the life of the church. The discovery of the empty tomb, the appearances of the Risen Jesus to the disciples, his words of comfort and his breaking of bread with them confirm what the entire Gospel has proclaimed: that Jesus is indeed the "Christ of God" whose obedient life and liberating mission are not in vain but fulfill God's plan of salvation. At the same time, they thrust the reader into Luke's presentation of the church and its founding impulse. The Risen Jesus implants his heritage with his disciples: they are to be witnesses to his gospel of repentance and forgiveness; they, too, must persevere through suffering and death; and, like Jesus, their liberating prophetic mission will be driven by the power of God's own Spirit.

[10]See D. Senior and C. Stuhlmueller, *The Biblical Foundations for Mission* (Maryknoll: Orbis, 1983) 255-79.

PART III

THE PASSION OF JESUS: LUKE'S MESSAGE

The Passion of Jesus in the Gospel of Luke is a drama that compels the reader's involvement in the mood and message of the story. Having seen the evangelist's preparation for the death of Jesus within the body of his Gospel, and having read through the Passion narrative itself in some detail, it is time to take stock of the fundamental currents that stir within Luke's account.

I. The Passion and Luke's Portrait of Jesus.

The dominant figure of the Passion story is, of course, Jesus himself. Through the Passion Luke expresses many of his basic convictions about the identity and mission of Jesus. Although we can attempt to sum up those convictions of the Gospel as separate statements, they are in fact closely intertwined.

Jesus is the Savior and liberating Messiah,
whose death for others brings the power
of God's forgiveness into the world.

Placing the saving power of Jesus' death at the head of the list runs counter to many interpretations of Luke's Gospel.[1]

---

[1]See the discussion above, pp. 135-37.

But reading through Luke's Passion story from start to finish, and viewing it in the light of his entire two volume work, lead to the conclusion that Luke views the death of Jesus as an integral part of his mission of salvation. Jesus' Passion and death, to be sure, are one part of his God-given destiny: that death leads organically to his resurrection, the resurrection to his triumphant exaltation with God, and that union with God to the gift of the Spirit on the church. By including in his two volume work the Passion account, resurrection appearances, a report of the Ascension, and the account of Pentecost, Luke reflects in his narrative on each phase of Jesus' passage from death to life.

Only with the completion of Jesus' mission and the descent of the Spirit are the full effects of salvation to be felt by the world. But the death of Jesus is not a mere way station along this epic process. The death of Jesus itself, because of who Jesus is and because of the manner of his dying, holds transforming power. Luke clearly illustrates this in the Passion story.

The link between the Passion and passover is one of the most important ways Luke interprets the death of Jesus as having saving, liberating power. The opening verse of the narrative sets the tone: on the eve of passover the enemies of Jesus gather to plot his death (22:1-2). Luke gives more attention to the passover meal than either Mark or Matthew (see 22:7-13, 14-38). Jesus' own words emphasize how important is this last meal before his death: "I have earnestly desired to eat this passover with you before I suffer" (22:15).

Passover was a liberation feast, an active remembrance of God's greatest act of salvation for Israel. The defeat of Pharaoh, the passage through the waters from slavery to freedom, the forging of the covenant at Sinai, the desert purification, and the gift of the land—all of these became the symbols of salvation for subsequent biblical history. That act of deliverance nourished Israel's enduring hope, even in moments of oppression and apparent hopelessness.

In Luke's Passion the memory of Passover and its ritual meal become the setting in which Jesus interprets the meaning of his death. Just as all of the Scriptures are fulfilled in

Jesus, so, too, is the meaning of this feast. The Passion of Jesus is the new passover, his death, a new exodus (9:31). The bread broken at the meal is Jesus' body "which is given for you" (22:25). The cup "poured out for you" is the forging of "a new covenant in my blood" (22:20). Only if one chooses to detach this entire scene from the Passion narrative and from the Gospel itself, can it be claimed that Luke does not interpret the death of Jesus as having saving power. To suggest that it reflects the "liturgical practice" of Luke's community, rather than a viewpoint the evangelist has thoroughly integrated into his theology, cannot be justified. In fact, Luke introduces his Passion narrative with this passover perspective. He presents Jesus himself interpreting his death as a death which will transform others. It is hard to imagine a more emphatic manner in which the evangelist could assert his theology.

Passover symbolism is not the only means Luke uses to interpret the death of Jesus as having the power to liberate from sin. As Jesus moves toward the climax of the Passion, acts of liberation and graciousness accelerate. The prayer of Jesus staves off the assault of Satan on Peter and the other disciples (22:31-32). In the garden the severed ear of the high priest's slave is healed (22:51). The look of his imprisoned master draws Peter back from the chasm of defeat and despair, and brings him to tears of repentance (22:61-62). Jesus forgives those who had just driven the cross spikes into his hands and feet (23:34). A repentant criminal is promised a home in paradise with the crucified Jesus on the very day of his death (23:43). The moment of Jesus' death brings a Roman Centurion to praise God and to confess that Jesus was indeed a "just man" (23:47). The sight of the cross stabs at the heart of the crowd who had passively agreed to Jesus' condemnation, and they return home "beating their breasts" in repentance (24:48). The magnetic power of the cross draws to it the weak and wavering disciples (23:49), and gives backbone to a member of the council that had condemned Jesus (23:50-52).

In each of these cases—all of them unique to Luke's Passion story—someone burdened with fear or weakness or evil is liberated from that burden by their proximity to the cross of Jesus. This is what Luke's Gospel understands by "forgiveness of sins." The term used (*apheis*) means literally the "lifting away" of sin, as in the summary of the gospel message given to the disciples by the Risen Christ: "repentance and forgiveness (*apheis*) of sins should be preached in (Jesus') name to all nations" (24:47).[2] "Forgiveness" thus understood is not exclusively a psychological or spiritual transformation but an act of liberation that touches every dimension of human existence. Healing, empowermemt, exorcism, befriending the poor and disenfranchised, speaking the truth— all of these characteristic actions of Jesus in the Gospel are expressions of liberation and forgiveness. They define what salvation means. So, too, do the acts of graciousness that course through the Passion story. Jesus is "reckoned with malefactors" (22:37), not, as his enemies supposed, because he was alienated from God but because his mission was to break the grip of death that held a weak and defenseless humanity captive. The final liberating act is Jesus' breaking of the power of death through the cross. This is the ultimate act of forgiveness and the events of transformation that cluster around it declare it so. Luke does not write discursive theology; his message is transmitted through narrative. What the reader sees is the impact of the death of Jesus on those close enough to experience its explosive force.

Another dimension of Luke's story helps interpret Jesus' death as a saving death. As we will discuss further below, Luke presents the Passion as the climactic struggle between Jesus and the power of evil. Suffering and death become Satan's opportunity to strike at Jesus, the holy one of God (22:3). In the biblical perspective, suffering and death are, ultimately, symptoms of evil's baffling grip on humanity. Luke, and indeed every New Testament writer, would subscribe to Paul's characterization of death as "the last enemy" (I Cor 15:26).

That terminal, pervasive grip of the demon death on hu-

---

[2]See above, pp. 157-58.

manity is broken by Jesus. In his genealogy Luke traces Jesus' origin back to the taproot of the human race: he is "Son of Adam" (3:38). Jesus is truly the representative human being, with all of the human drama and all human hopes caught up in his very person. Jesus, in effect, is the "New Adam," the new human being who inaugurates a new and decisive age of salvation for humanity.[3] Jesus' obedience—in contrast to the sinfulness of the first Adam—wins for humanity access to God. Because he is the "new human being," the "Son of Adam," Jesus is not exempt from suffering and death but his obedience achieves a new breakthrough. Therefore in the Passion story Jesus is immersed in the struggle with death and must pray to God for strength and deliverance (22:42). The power of darkness tears at Jesus in the guise of Judas' betrayal, in the fear and weakness of Peter and the apostles, in the relentless hatred of the leaders, in Herod's treacherous corruption, in Pilate's fatal placating of the crowd, in the repeated taunts and mockeries that clutch at Jesus until the moment of death, in the fury of nature itself as the sun darkens and the veil before the sanctuary of the temple is destroyed. Luke presents Jesus passing through the Passion as if through some nightmare guantlet, with a thousand furies attempting to humiliate and defeat him.

But Jesus, the savior and liberator, God's champion and strong one, is not defeated by the demonic power of death. He experiences death to the full but his spirit is given to God not to Satan. Through his unbreakable bond of trust with God, Jesus goes through the experience of death but is not destroyed. In a very true sense, the drama of salvation is enacted in Jesus himself. This was his God-given destiny. Repeatedly Luke emphasizes this in his Gospel: "The Christ

[3]This theme of the "New Adam" is given major emphasis by J. Neyrey (*The Passion According to Luke*, esp. 156-92), perhaps with some exaggeration. He concedes that this theme, which is very overt in Paul's theology, is only intimated in Luke. The only explicit reference to Adam is in 3:38. But such events as the temptation of Jesus (4:1-13, with its echoes in the Gethsemani scene, 22:39-46, and the mockeries at the cross, 23:35-38), and the promise of paradise to the repentant criminal (23:43) indicate that it is close to the surface of Luke's theology.

must suffer these things and so enter into his glory" (24:26).[4] That destiny is not a grimless fate, but a consequence of Jesus' trust in God and free commitment to God's will.

Because he carries through on his journey to the cross, Jesus fulfills his role as the promised Messiah. His royal identity had been proclaimed from the first pages of the Gospel.[5] As the Christ, the anointed King, Jesus pours out his life rallying and nourishing God's people. And, once again, the climax of his messianic mission comes in the Passion. Here irony plays a heavy role in the drama. While his opponents attempt to portray Jesus as a foolish pretender for political power (23:2, 5), the reader knows the real truth of Jesus' royal dignity. The proof of Jesus' identity as the "Christ, God's Chosen one" is not, as his taunters imagine, the ability to save himself (23:35), but precisely the pouring out of his life for others. When his executioners fix the placard to the top of the cross—"This is the King of the Jews" (23:38)—it is meant as another nail of mockery and ridicule driven into the hopes of this pitiful messianic pretender. But the reader knows this *is* the Christ, the King, the source of hope for Jew and Gentile alike.

Jesus is the Son of God who trusts completely in God and is faithful to God through death; he is the Just One whom even death itself cannot separate from God.

The experience of suffering and death can, in a paradoxical way, bring illumination. In the shadow of death, shallow relationships fall away, the true values of our deepest soul well up to the surface, and the rare treasures of life and fidelity stand out luminously. The Passion narrative of Luke presents Jesus as immersed in such a crisis of the human spirit. Particularly important are the prayers of Jesus that occur within the passion. The spirit and content of Jesus' prayers in crisis reveal the identity of Jesus as understood by the evangelist.

---

[4]See above, Part I, pp. 35-36.
[5]See above, 109-11.

A key title for Jesus throughout the Gospel and one that comes to the fore in the context of the Passion is "Son of God."[6] The title "Son of God" has several connotations in the biblical world, referring to the king, and used by extension as a reference to the faithful Israelite. Under the influence of Greek culture, the term can also imply a sharing in divine power.[7] All of these nuances shade the meaning of the term in Luke, but particularly important is the connotation of Jesus' closeness to God because of his trust and obedience. That bond was tested by Satan in the desert (4.1-13), and once more in the Passion drama itself (see, especially, 22:70). The full sweep of Luke's drama is taken up with this enduring relationship between Jesus and his God, from the Spirit's infusion of life in the womb of Mary until the triumphant return of the Risen Christ to the right hand of his Father.

The Passion prayers of Jesus reveal this core truth of the Gospel. Three times Jesus cries to his Father in prayer, revealing his communion with God and reaffirming his trust. The first instance is the prayer before Jesus' arrest (22:39-46): "Father, if thou art willing, remove this cup from me; nevertheless not my will, but thine, be done." This prayer is the outer expression of Jesus' inner identity as Son of God. He pleads for strength and deliverance in the face of death, but the foundation of the prayer is Jesus' unswerving loyalty to God.[8]

As he is nailed to the cross, another prayer is wrenched from Jesus' lips: "Father, forgive them; for they know not what they do" (23:34). This prayer is not simply a reflex of compassion and mercy on Jesus' part; in the context of Luke's entire Gospel, it is the plea of Jesus the savior reaffirming his mission from God: "forgive them." Because Jesus is bonded in trust and obedience with a God of un-

---

[6]See above, 22:70.

[7]See M. Hengel, *The Son of God* (Philadelphia: Fortress, 1976); J. Dunn, *Christology in the Making* (Philadelphia: Westminster, 1980), 12-64; R. Fuller & P. Perkins, *Who is This Christ? Gospel Christology and Contemporary Faith* (Philadelphia: Fortress, 1983), 41-82.

[8]See above, pp. 84-89.

limited compassion, he is able to pray for his enemies (6:27-36).[9]

Jesus' final prayer is the most revealing: "Father, into thy hands I commit my spirit!" (23:46). These final words of the earthly Jesus tell the full meaning of the "Son of God" title in Luke. Jesus is "son" because he is willing to entrust his entire being to God, even as death pulls at that relationship and seeks to put it in doubt. Here another, allied, biblical tradition is invoked by Luke. The wisdom tradition of the suffering just one (also called "Son of God" as in Wisdom 2:13, 16, 18; 5:5) reflected on the mystery of trust under assault. This figure of the Israelite who trusts in God yet is nearly overwhelmed by suffering and isolation haunts many of the lament psalms and the early chapters of the Wisdom of Solomon.[10] As Jesus approaches the threshold of death, he, too, is mocked as the just one of Israel was (23:25-39). But his last word is not despair or bitterness, but complete trust. As darkness snuffs out the light of the sun, and the veil of the temple is torn apart, Jesus, true child of God, places his battered spirit into the hands of his Father.

Such trust is not misplaced. God hears the voice of those who cry out in faith and agony. The signs of victory and affirmation begin to explode in Luke's account with increasing tempo: the Roman Centurion who executed Jesus is transformed, praises God, and acclaims Jesus as truly the "just one" (23:47); the crowd repents (23:48); a member of the council that condemned him takes courage and does homage to this just man (23:50-56); those who come to the tomb find it empty (24:1-12); and on the road and in the city, the Risen Jesus reveals himself alive to his followers (24:13-49). The Gospel ends with Jesus, who had entrusted his spirit to his Father, lifted up in glory (24:51).

There is little doubt that through the account of Passion and glory, Luke proclaims to his church the most profound

---

[9]On the connection of this prayer with the love of enemies command, see above, pp. 128-29.

[10]See, for example, Psalms 22, 42, 43, 61, 116, etc., and Wisdom chapters 2 to 5.

truth about Jesus. At the same time, he lays bare his conviction that faith in God is not misplaced. God is trustworthy and death cannot discredit God.

*Jesus is the prophet-martyr who fearlessly proclaims
God's justice, giving faithful witness even in the face
of rejection and death.*

That Luke portrays Jesus as a prophet was clear from the opening pages of the Gospel.[11] The appealing Jewish characters of the infancy narrative are all animated by lavish portions of God's Spirit. Jesus' own conception is a pure gift of the Creator Spirit at work in Mary (1:35). That same Spirit infuses Jesus himself at his baptism (3:22) and would drive him into his ministry (4:14). In the synagogue of Nazareth (4:18-19), Jesus, the Spirit-anointed prophet, would take to himself Isaiah's proclamation of justice.[12] And commitment to that mission of justice would be evident in the days of teaching, healing, and conflicts that fill the mission of Jesus in Luke's Gospel.

Wearing the mantle of prophecy meant earning opposition and rejection, and the Gospel makes no secret of this. Jesus' befriending of the poor and the oppressed caused scandal and offense. His boundary-breaking ministry would be resisted. His challenge to warped values and arbitrary exclusion would enkindle anger and resentment. Luke's Jesus is fully aware that he walks the same fateful journey taken by the prophets of old:

> "Nevertheless I must go on my way today and tomorrow and the day following; for it cannot be that a prophet should perish away from Jerusalem. O Jerusalem, Jerusalem, killing the prophets and stoning those who are sent to you! How often would I have gathered your children together as a hen gathers her brood under her wings, and you would not!" (13:33-34).

[11]See Part I, pp. 28-31

[12]On this key scene, see above, pp. 18-21.

That same mix of fearless public witness to justice and compassion, and sharp rejection because of it is found in the Passion story. In the city of Jerusalem, Jesus the prophet would meet death. But the manner of his dying would proclaim anew his prophetic message. As discussed earlier, Luke's Passion story cannot be reduced to a martyrdom story.[13] But this motif has a strong part to play. There is a confident, almost muscular tone to Luke's presentation of the Passion. On the eve of passover Jesus is fully aware of what is in store for him. He directs the preparation of the passover meal (22:8) and instructs his disciples on the meaning of his death and the shape of their own destiny (22:14-38). As the decisive hour of the arrest approaches, there is a moment of acute testing. As a martyr Jesus struggles with impending death, begging God for the strength to endure it (22:39-46).[14] Fortified by God's grace (visibly communicated in Luke's account by an "angel from heaven," 22:43), Jesus stands up from his prayer and faces the power of darkness. Judas' attempt to kiss him is deflected (22:48): Jesus the prophet knows the heart of his betrayer. The guards mock his claim to prophetic power (22:63-65) but when accused by the Sanhedrin, Jesus speaks boldly, without flinching (22:67-70). He replies to the question of the Roman Governor (23:3) but ignores Herod and the chorus of accusations from the leaders (23:6-12). When the crowds and the women of Jerusalem lament his fate, he utters a prophetic oracle, warning them of their own threatening destiny (23:27-31). And when death comes, Jesus dies with confidence, entrusting his spirit to the God who gave it (23:46).

Throughout this measured march to death, Jesus the prophet gives witness to God's mercy and justice—just as he had done on the great journey from Galilee to Jerusalem.[15] He proclaims God's compassion in rejecting violence and healing

---

[13]See above, 145, n. 37.

[14]This interpretation is emphasized by R. Barbour, "Gethsemane in the Tradition of the Passion," *New Testament Studies* 16 (1969/70) 231-51.

[15]See above, Part I, pp. 35-39.

the severed ear of his enemy (22:51). His look of compassion saves Peter (22:61) and he forgives his executioners (23:34). As he had done throughout his mission, he sides with the "malefactors" in accepting the last minute homage of a dying criminal (23:43).

The rejection that hounded Jesus in his public ministry comes to term here. He is taunted for claiming to be a prophet (22:63), his identity as Christ and Son of God are rejected (22:71), his disturbing mission of liberation misconstrued as hunger for political power (23:2,5); his commitment to save and to heal is mocked (23:35-39). Even the crowds who had hung on his words and praised God for his graciousness turn on him and join the chorus of rejection (23:18, 21, 23). Jesus the prophet experienced the terrible destiny of those who proclaim God's word without compromise.

But the reader of Luke's Gospel knows the outcome of this drama. The word of God cannot be stilled. The prophetic voice will be heard and prove life-giving, even though people attempt to suppress it. The resurrection of Jesus and his ascent to God are the validation of Jesus' prophetic vocation. "God raised him up, having loosed the pangs of death, because it was not possible for him to be held by it." (Acts 2:24).[16]

II. The Passion and the Power of Darkness

In the Passion of Jesus the ultimate drama of good and evil, of life and death is enacted. Through his death and resurrection Jesus, the representative human being, defines human destiny.

More than the other evangelists, Luke links the power of death with ultimate evil. As we noted in Part I, Luke introduces this motif at the beginning of the Gospel. Evil in the person of Satan stalks Jesus in the desert (4:1-13), and

[16]On Luke's vindication theology, see above, pp. 102-103.

through repeated conflicts and exorcisms in the course of his ministry, the tenacious hostility of demonic evil is present.[17]

But the definitive battleground was to be the Passion. After exhausting his efforts to seduce Jesus in the desert, Satan leaves "for an opportune time" (4:13). That time comes with the Passion, as Satan enters into Judas and the terrible mechanism of treachery and death clicks on (22:3). Evil's threatening presence weaves through the story, masked with a human face: Judas' senseless betrayal, the disciples' weakness, the implacable hostility of the leaders, the crowd's compliance, Herod's leering curiosity, Pilate's indecision and ultimate injustice, the hailstorm of taunts for a dying man.

That there is more here than human weakness and miscalculation is signaled by Jesus' own words. He warns his disciples that in his approaching Passion he faces the "test"— the *peirasmos*—the ultimate struggle foreseen in the Scriptures between life and death, between goodness and evil (22:28, 36, 40, 46). As his enemies press forward to arrest him, Jesus identifies the real driving force of their hatred: "This is your hour, and the power of darkness" (22:53). And finally when death stepped forward as if to claim its prize, the sun is eclipsed and the earth is shrouded in darkness, and the veil before God's sanctuary was torn in two—cosmic signs of evil's oppressive strength (22:44-45).

In this way, Luke pays homage to the terrible power of death. Even though Luke has Jesus in control of his destiny, in this narrative there is no underestimation of the baffling and aggressive role of evil and suffering in human experience. At the same time, the full scope of the Passion story leaves no doubt that ultimate evil is defeated. It seems to exhaust its fury on Jesus, God's son. Through the power of God's love, the power of death is sapped—for all time and for all people.

The full narration of that victory takes the reader into the resurrection stories and into the triumphant life of the community described in Acts. But even in the Passion story Luke

---

[17]See above, Part I, pp. 31-35.

gives signs of that ultimate victory. The triumph of grace over death can be seen in the ambivalence of those targeted by the power of evil. The disciples who are weak and uncomprehending will gradually find their courage and become the Risen Christ's witnesses (24:48). The crowds who condemn Jesus also are moved to weep for him (23:27) and repent at the sight of his death (23:48). One criminal mocks Jesus but the other clings to him for hope and is rewarded with a share in paradise (23:43). The Roman Centurion who presides over Jesus' death is the first to recognize his justice (23:47). Joseph, a member of the Council that condemned Jesus, finds the courage to claim the body of the Crucified (23:50-53). Jerusalem, that ambivalent city—site of God's house and murderer of prophets (13:34-35), place of prayer and vision (1-2), place of rejection and crucifixion (22-23)—is itself a sign in Luke's Gospel of the struggle between good and evil. The city where death seems to crush the child of God is the very place where the Spirit sent by the Risen Christ will take root (Luke 24:49; Acts 1:8).

By having the drama of life and death played out in the Passion of Jesus, Luke proclaims the fullest meaning of the Gospel. In Jesus —Son of God, Son of Adam—all of humanity's hope is represented. The outcome of Jesus' encounter with evil and death is the forecast of all human destiny. Injustice, suffering, death are severe realities, the Passion story acknowledges, but they do not have final power over human life.

III. The Passion and the Community

In the experience of the Passion, the meaning and challenge of authentic discipleship are revealed.

There is little doubt that each evangelist intended the Passion drama as an instruction on discipleship. In the arena of death one's true responses are revealed. That is clearly the case in Luke's Passion story. The reactions of the disciples and other characters in the drama instruct the reader on what following Jesus means and at what cost.

Because Luke portrays Jesus' Passion as a struggle and a "test," the value of perseverance becomes a key point of discipleship instruction. The focus falls especially on the "apostles" in Luke.[18] This core group called by Jesus and sent out on mission are to walk with him from Galilee to Jerusalem and, after his resurrection, to be the core community from which would radiate the explosive mission of the Spirit (Acts 1:8). "Following after" Jesus (23:26) and "staying with him" (22:28), therefore, are key metaphors for discipleship. The journey of Jesus with his followers that spans much of Luke's Gospel reaches its decisive stage in Jerusalem.[19] The Passion—with its mix of suffering and threat, its call for vigilance and public choice—becomes the testing ground for the apostles' perseverance.

Luke's portrayal of the disciples is realistic. Although Luke does not emphasize the weakness of the disciples in the Passion story as emphatically as Mark, it would be inaccurate to claim that he idealizes them. Reference to their sleep during Jesus' anguished prayer may be softened (see 22:45-46), and Luke does not directly refer to their flight at the moment of the arrest (22:54; compare Mark 14:51-52). But in other ways Luke's portrayal is as unflattering as any of the Gospels. At the passover meal the apostles argue about their own greatness just as Jesus proclaims his self-sacrificing death (22:24). Peter rashly pledges unswerving loyalty in the face of Jesus' prediction that Satan hungered for the apostle's soul (22:31-34). When Jesus warns the disciples to arm themselves for the struggle with evil that lay ahead, they misunderstand his words (22:35-38). While Jesus prays vigilantly for strength and urges his disciples to do the same, they succumb to fear and fall sleep (22:39-46). In the moment of crisis, one of the disciples uses a sword—directly violating Jesus' teaching about non-retaliation (22:49-51). And when the climax of

[18]See above, Part I, pp. 71-75.

[19]See above, Part I, pp. 35-39. Although the journey from Galilee to Jerusalem ends with the entry into the holy city (19:45), a cosmic dimension of that journey continues as Jesus moves through death to exaltation. Luke refers to Jesus' death-resurrection as his being "received up" (9:51).

the Passion story arrives and Jesus entrusts his spirit to God, the "friends" of Jesus are a weak and distant presence at the cross (23:49).

Thus Luke is not afraid to portray Jesus' own disciples, who would be the nucleus of the Spirit filled community in Acts, as weak and in dire need of repentance. Peter himself displays this whole spectrum. The first of Jesus' disciples to be called, Peter himself recognizes that he is a "sinful man" (5:8). In the Passion that weakness is in full display. Despite his bravado in promising "to go with [Jesus] to prison and to death" (22:33), he three times denies his relationship to Jesus (22:54-62). And his confusion and doubts will linger even when he sees the empty tomb (24:12).

Through the Passion story Luke warns his community that persecution, suffering, and witness unto death would take their toll. To proclaim the gospel of justice Jesus embodied would not be without cost. That is why calls to vigilance and earnest prayer echo through the story. Because of the very nature of the Gospel and the world's instinctive resistance to it, the follower of Jesus needed to be alert and ready for the assault of evil (22:36). One should be ready to travel light, yet with the needed resources (22:35-38). Praying for strength is a special plea of Luke's account. Jesus himself models such a prayer on the Mount of Olives (22:41-42) and the disciples are urged to pray in the same manner (22:40, 46). Only because of such prayer on Jesus' part would Simon and the other disciples survive the test (22:31-32).

The passover meal is another clue to Luke's notion of discipleship.[20] In the breaking of the bread and the sharing of the cup, Jesus instructed them on the meaning of his death as a servant death for others (22:19-20, 27). The manner of Jesus' life-giving service for others was to be the model for the disciples' own ministry (22:25-27). Jesus' own person—his life, his mission, his word—would feed his disciples and draw them together in vital communion. That nourishing process takes place at the passover meal and would be re-

---

[20]See above, pp. 56-58.

peated in the post-easter meals of the Risen Christ with his
followers.[21]

The inclusive nature of Jesus' meals in the Gospel also
comes into play here. Meals within the kingdom established
by Jesus were open to the poor, the disenfranchised, the
disabled (14:12-24).[22] Even in the Passion story, this inclusive
nature of Jesus' community is apparent. The disciples' self-
absorption and hunger for power that erupts at the passover
meal is checked by Jesus, and they are reminded that they
are to be as "those who serve" (22:26-27). At that same meal
Jesus accepts the label his enemies throw at him—"reckoned
with transgressors"—and will later go to his death in the
company of criminals (22:37; 23:43). And clustered around
the cross are a converted Roman soldier, crowds of repentant
Jews, and the battered friends of Jesus (23:47-49). These are
the very kind of people who will take heart through the
Spirit's power and ultimately form the community in Acts.
The apostles will be the leaders of that community; Jesus
had promised this at the passover meal: "I assign to you, as
my Father assigned to me, a kingdom, that you may eat and
drink at my table in my kingdom, and sit on thrones judging
the twelve tribes of Israel" (22:29-30). But that exercise of
leadership would come about, as Jesus had warned Peter,
only after the power of Jesus' prayer had snatched them
from evil and turned them back from weakness to strength
(22:32).

As noted earlier, Luke portrays Jesus as the prophet-
martyr, whose courageous encounter with death in the cause
of justice is meant to give public witness to the gospel. This is
apparent in the Passion story, where Jesus acts fearlessly and
with integrity. In the depth of his Passion, he heals and
forgives and gives courageous testimony.

Without doubt Luke intends this as instruction for the
disciples. Giving witness is an important quality of authentic
discipleship in Luke's theology. The final words of the Risen

[21]See above, pp 155-58.
[22]See above, pp. 73-74.

Christ commission them: "You are witnesses of these things" (24:48).[23] But within the Passion story the disciples act without courage. They sleep out of fear at the moment of crisis (22:45), display values opposed to the gospel such as self-aggrandizement (22:24) and violence (22:49-50) and fade from view as the Passion reaches its climax. Peter, in fact, becomes the negative exponent of gospel witness: publicly denying his discipleship at the very moment Jesus proclaims before the Sanhedrin his own identity as Christ and Son of God (22:54-71).

Paradoxically, the only public witness given on behalf of the Gospel other than by Jesus himself comes not from the apostles but from minor and unexpected characters of the drama. Simon of Cyrene carries the cross behind Jesus (23:26); the Jerusalem crowds and the daughters of Jerusalem lament Jesus' condemnation (23:28); a condemned criminal asks for salvation from Jesus (23:42); the Roman centurion proclaims his identity as God's just one (23:47); Joseph of Arimathea and the women from Galilee claim his body and see to his burial (23:50-56). These, and not the Twelve, offer some degree of public witness concerning Jesus and the gospel within the Passion story.

The Passion story is rich in irony. The weak are strong and the strong are weak. The one who dies in apparent defeat is the one who lives triumphant. In the case of the apostles—weak and failing in the glare of the Passion, yet still called to witness and leadership—one can surmise that Luke's ironies were intended to challenge, and encourage, his community.

IV. The Passion and the Meaning of Death.

The early community's reflection on the death of Jesus by means of the Passion narratives gives insight into their understanding of death itself. Jesus' encounter with death absorbs

[23]See above, pp. 157-58.

the entire human family's experience of this mysterious reality.

Through the subtle and unique shadings within their Passion narratives, each evangelist gives a different perspective on the mystery of death. No single New Testament author exhausts the meaning of death but each is instructive. Luke's Passion story has its own peculiar wisdom on the experience of death.

Death is a struggle and test leading to a profound experience of liberation and life.

The death of Jesus exemplifies that suffering and death can be understood as a struggle that shakes the foundation of the human spirit. Suffering and death can come as an aggressive enemy, seeking to "sift" and disillusion the human spirit, even to destroy it. Death is viewed here as "enemy" of life; as an expression of ultimate evil, that tests every conviction and every relationship.

There is no romanticism here, no winking at the tragedy of death. Because it is in the context of the Passion story and of the Gospel itself, however, neither is there despair. Death is given its due, but so is God's power. Luke's Passion story triumphantly proclaims that one can pass through the test of suffering and death to new and profound life. That is the testimony of Jesus' own experience, the paschal mystery that is the foundation of all Christian hope.

Death is the culmination point of a life-long journey to God.

The long view of Luke's two volume work presents death as the last milestone on Jesus' journey to God. His entire life's mission is cast in the form of a journey stretching from Galilee to Jerusalem, from the Passion to the glory of life with God. Jesus' death is also swept up in this rich metaphor. At the same time it is a struggle, the Passion of Jesus is also a sure stepping stone from a life oriented to God to life in full communion with God. In a strange way, the Passion is Jesus' destiny—he "had to suffer"—because suffering and death were astride the path that led home.

Here, too, is a realistic, and touchingly human, view of death. Death is part of the human journey; all must take this road, even if its turns are unknown and forbidding. The Gospel that encloses this journey motif prevents it from being another expression of blind fate or meaninglessness. The journey does not end with death; it leads home to God. And once again faith in the Risen Christ is the foundation for such hope. Jesus experiences his own "exodus," his own "going up"; his journey from death to life becomes the pattern for all journeys in faith.

Death as opportunity for witness

Many, perhaps most, Christian deaths seem to present little opportunity for public "witness." Death in a hospital: gradual, inevitable, aseptic, out of control of family or friends. Death by accident: unintended, unexpected, unwitnessed. Often death comes without any apparent place for heroic example to be given or received.

Yet Luke's Gospel presents Jesus' Passion as a public spectacle which has profound impact on those present. Jesus' sufferings and his reactions to them are heroic. What he says and what he does as death approaches is in full harmony with his own teaching and life commitments. In the crucible of suffering and death such integrity gives a powerful witness to the Gospel.

In an age when public Christian witness in the midst of suffering and death is a common experience for many churches throughout the world, Luke's Passion story has increasing importance. Martyrdom, understood as suffering and death on behalf of the Gospel, can be a profound expression of discipleship and is often the most eloquent proclamation of the Gospel possible. Luke's Passion narrative retains that important memory for the church. And even for those whose death may appear more passive and not the result of commitment to the Gospel, the Lukan story of Jesus' martyr's death reminds the church that goodness and patience and fidelity carried out over a lifetime and into the quiet mystery of death also proclaim the Gospel of Jesus' triumph and give a witness of hope.

Subject Index

Author Index

Scripture Index